ASSEMBLY AUTOPSY

Andrew W. Wilson

Assembly Autopsy: Why Brethren Churches are Dying and How to Revive Them.

Copyright © 2023 Andrew Wilson

Believers Publications, P. O. Box 485, North Lakes, Queensland, 4509, Australia

All rights reserved. No part of this publication may be reproduced or transmitted in any form or by any means, electronic or mechanical, including photocopy, recording or otherwise, except for brief quotations in printed reviews, without the written permission of the publisher.

Scripture quotations, unless otherwise noted, are taken from the New King James Version, copyright © 1979, 1980, 1982 by Thomas Nelson, Inc. Used by permission. All rights reserved.

Scripture quotations marked (KJV) are taken from The Holy Bible, Authorized King James Version

Scripture quotations marked (NIV) are taken from the Holy Bible, New International Version®, NIV®, copyright © 1973, 1978, 1984, 2011 by Biblica, Inc.™ Used by permission of Zondervan. All rights reserved worldwide. www.zondervan.com The "NIV" and "New International Version" are registered in the United States Patent and Trademark Office by Biblica, Inc.™.

ISBN: 978-0-9943977-8-2

CONTENTS

	Introductory Note	v
1	Assemblies in the West are Dying	1
2	Who are the Brethren?	15
3	How Recovery Begins	55
4	How God Works	71
5	How to Produce Healthy Christians	85
6	How to Resuscitate Struggling Churches	115
7	The Source of the Power	138
8	How to Care for the Flock	166
9	The Supreme Virtue	189
10	Conclusion	203
	Endnotes	205

INTRODUCTORY NOTE

This book is about so-called 'Brethren assemblies'. Most people in the 'Brethren' do not like to use the name to describe themselves. But from very early on, the label was used by others outside the movement, and the name stuck. The word 'assemblies' is used by many Brethren as another word for 'churches'. Here in this book, I use the names 'Brethren' and 'assemblies' as a short-hand way of referring to these churches. If any are offended by the word 'autopsy' (a medical examination of a body to determine the cause of death), I ask their forgiveness – I come from a medical family.

For those who ask what credentials I have to write this book, I was commended to full-time ministry from Bexley Christian Assembly in Sydney, Australia, in 1994, and this is my thirtieth year serving the Lord among Brethren assemblies, both in England and Australia. During that time I have been involved in helping struggling local churches as well as ones doing well, both among conservative assemblies and among some not quite so conservative. I have also been involved in itinerant ministry, teaching in many places, from small meetings to large conferences. For five years, I did part-time study and research in the Greek New Testament at Tyndale House, Cambridge, England, as a result of which I have published a number of articles in the academic literature. Most years I teach New Testament Greek, as well as training a group of younger preachers. I lectured for some years at the GLO Discipleship Training School in

Smithton, Tasmania on Systematic Theology. I also write the occasional expository article in *Precious Seed* magazine. I am the author of eight other books, including *Matthew's Messiah: a Guide to Matthew's Gospel*, *Why There Really is a God, and What You Need to Know about Him*, *Do Not Quench the Spirit: a Biblical and Practical Guide to Participatory Church Gatherings*, and *The End of the World: What the Bible Says about the Future*.

My family's history among the Brethren goes back well over one hundred years. My grandfather on my mother's side, William Bunting, was a leading Irish evangelist and Bible teacher. My other grandfather, Victor Wilson, left Northern Ireland with the intention of being a medical missionary in China. As a result of the Chinese communist take-over in 1949, he settled in Australia, hoping that the way might open for missionary work later. It did not, and as a result, I grew up in Australia. My wife is the daughter of an English Brethren full-time worker, who was himself the grandson of an Irish evangelist, Edward Hughes (1857-1944, see *Irish Evangelists now with the Lord*). My wife and I have four children and live in northern New South Wales, Australia.

Ultimately, our trust must be in God's Word. Test the prescription given here against Scripture. 'To the law and the testimony! If they do not speak according to this word, it is because there is no light in them' (Isa. 8:20). God's Word alone contains the solutions to the challenges we face today. 'Trust in the LORD with all your heart, and lean not on your own understanding' (Prov. 3:5).

Chapter One

ASSEMBLIES IN THE WEST ARE DYING

It was 1993, and I had just arrived in London, England, from Australia. It was at the end of October, and I was experiencing a little bit of culture shock. In Australia, we have bright, warm sunshine for three-quarters of the year, but in London I had two straight weeks of cold, grey and gloomy weather – it neither rained nor did the sun break through. I didn't know anyone in this vast, bustling, murky, multicultural city that I felt God had called me to.

There was one place in England that I particularly wanted to visit: Brook Street Chapel in Tottenham, London. Just before I had left Australia, I received a letter from a distant relative who had heard that I was coming to England. She thought that I was going to live in London, and recommended that I attend Brook Street Chapel, Tottenham. Before coming to England I had no desire to stay for any time in London. So I didn't pay much attention to this letter until the Sunday before I was due to leave, when we had our Sunday School prizegiving, and I was reading through one of the books I was giving out to my teenage Bible class. It was a biography of Hudson Taylor, and in it he told how he visited Brook Street Chapel in Tottenham in the 1830s before going to

China as a missionary. When I read this, I went and spoke to my father, and asked him whether the Brook Street Chapel mentioned by Hudson Taylor could possibly be the same place that our relative had mentioned in her letter. To my surprise, my Dad told me that it was the same place, and a Brethren assembly that he himself had visited in the 1960s when he was studying in London.

I was stunned. Three times in the space of little more than a week, just before I was due to leave home, and not knowing where in England I was meant to go, I had come across Brook Street Chapel, Tottenham. Although I didn't really want to stay in London, God seemed to be nudging me in that direction. I thought I would at least have to go one Sunday and visit Brook Street Chapel.

It turned out that Brook Street Chapel was one of the oldest assemblies in the world, founded in the 1830s. There were about 20-30 believers in fellowship. I ended up staying a year there, helping two inner-city evangelists as they preached the gospel. It proved to be a very good training ground for me as a young Christian. Every month we would conduct a week-long children's mission in an assembly either in London or out in the country. As a result, I saw quite a few assemblies in and around London. During one of these children's missions, I found an old assembly address book. It was from the period after the Second World War, and it listed over 100 assemblies in the greater London area (I counted them). This greatly surprised me because, from what I could tell, there were now far less than this number still counted as Brethren assemblies in the greater London area. I was shocked:

what had happened to all these assemblies?

Some of the older believers at Tottenham told me stories of days gone by, when there were four assemblies in Tottenham, when they had over 200 children in the Sunday School, and forty Sunday School teachers, so that they had to hire an entire train to take the children on their yearly Sunday School picnic to the seaside.

Over the next few years (I came back to England and spent two more years in Tottenham later in my twenties) I saw at first hand the closure of many other assemblies in the greater London area. Of the assemblies we went and helped (either with children's outreaches or with occasional preaching), I know of about 10 that have closed over the last 25 years.

One of the most famous assemblies in north London was at Clapton Hall, Stoke Newington. Around the beginning of the 20th century it had so many members (some reports say 700) that people were asked to write their name on a piece of paper and put it in a box at the front door every Sunday, so that the elders would know who had been present. This assembly had closed in the early 1990s just before I arrived in England, and the building was boarded up, awaiting conversion into flats. Seeing I had to walk past this suburb to get from my lodgings to Tottenham, I decided to go and have a look at the building one day. I managed to get in through the flimsy fence erected around the building by the property developers and looked inside the empty building. Sure enough, as I had been told, its massive auditorium had a long sloping floor so that people at the back of the hall would be able to see the speaker at the front.

While Brethren have historically 'manifested a supreme lack of interest in their numerical strength'[1], indifference no longer seems appropriate. Roy Hill, who published the UK Assemblies Address book, in a 2005 article titled 'What is Happening to UK Assemblies?' wrote that by the mid-20th century (at their peak numerically) there were about 1800 assemblies in the United Kingdom, with as many as 100,000 members. But:

> by the end of 2003 the number [of assemblies] had reduced to around 1158 assemblies (705 in England, 195 in Scotland, 173 in N. Ireland and 75 in Wales) with perhaps only about 40,000 members between them, a huge drop of 36% in assemblies and 60% in members in 40 years! But, alarmingly, in the last few years assemblies have been 'closing' at the rate of about one per week, and the numbers in some of those remaining are very few indeed[2].

By 2014, the next edition of the Assembly Address book, the number had dropped by 30% to 828 (433 in England, 173 in Scotland, 161 in N. Ireland and 61 in Wales).

The *Brethren Movement Worldwide, Key Information* 2019 edition listed 540 congregations in England, 150 in Northern Ireland, 150 in Scotland, and 61 in Wales. Whichever way we count them, the number of assemblies is declining. Neil Summerton writes, 'Since 1960 the number of assemblies and churches associated with the Brethren movement in the UK has halved ... There is a real risk that the movement will cease to have effective existence in the UK in the next generation"[3].

In 2009, my wife and I visited Dublin. One of the sights that I cannot forget is Merrion Hall, a stone's throw from Ireland's main parliament square. Merrion Hall was probably the largest Brethren Gospel Hall ever built, with seating capacity of nearly 3000 in the very heart of the city. It had been modelled on Spurgeon's Tabernacle in London and had three levels of galleries. It was built in 1863, after the great revival that swept the British Isles. In the late 1980s the grand old building was sold to a developer. It is now a luxury hotel.

It is not just in the United Kingdom that assemblies are closing at an alarming rate. One of the results of the 1859 revival was wave after wave of missionaries and evangelists from the British Isles who went out into all the world with the gospel message. In the 1870s God brought revival through three evangelists (an Englishman, a Scotsman and an Irishman) to the north coast of Tasmania, Australia[4]. This work continued to be blessed with converts and new assemblies into the 1930s. After my grandfather emigrated from Ireland to live in Australia in the late 1940s, he travelled down to Tasmania in the 1950s. Every weekend in the summer holidays there was a conference at one town after another along the north coast, with many hundreds attending. Nowadays virtually all these conferences have ceased. I was told by an old farmer a few years ago that, at their height (numerically), there were 50 assemblies along the north coast of Tasmania. Now there are less than 20. Many of these remaining are small and struggling.

I grew up in Sydney, where the oldest assembly, founded in the 1850s, closed a few years ago. In the middle of the 20th century, the assembly was quite large and met in a grand old Salvation Army citadel in the centre of the city: Goulburn Street Gospel Hall, with balcony seating on a second level. This assembly closed a few years ago, but before that sad event it had to move out of the Gospel Hall to smaller premises. For some years after the assembly vacated the building, it was used as an adult (i.e. pornographic) cinema. Another assembly near where I grew up in Sydney closed a few years before, and the Gospel Hall is now an Islamic Mosque.

At their peak, numerically, in the mid-to-late 1980s, there were about 265 Australian assemblies listed in Australian Missionary Tidings Notice of Meetings. In 2015, this number had dropped to 201 assemblies. During those 25 years, 65 assemblies – about one quarter of the total – closed in Australia[5].

The same story – of old buildings, where God once brought great blessing, now sold off and used for other purposes – is being repeated in many other places. Where God once brought revival, there is now very little left.

Now, please understand that when I speak of assemblies dying, I am referring to Western countries. In many places in the developing world, particularly in India and Africa, Brethren assemblies are growing. For example, in the last ten years, the number of assemblies has increased in Chad from about 1000 to nearly 2000, in Ethiopia from about 80 to over 250, in Nigeria from about 800 to over 1200, and in India from over 2000 to over 4000[6]. But in the West, things are either stationary, or in the UK and other countries, in decline.

One apparent exception is North America, where the number of assemblies is stable or gradually increasing[7]. But even these numbers may be masking deeper problems. Dr. Alex Kurian, who has served the Lord for over 40 years, in India and the United States, says that decline is happening even in North America. In personal correspondence, Dr. Kurian tells me that although there are stable assemblies in the USA, there is little growth from gospel outreach, and many assemblies are only surviving because of immigrants, especially from India. In an internet article, *The Decline of the Assemblies*, he writes:

> In places where the Brethren were very influential and numerically strong with high profile spiritual leaders, and vibrant congregations, they are barely surviving with one or two halls here and there, with very few in number, mainly 3-4 elderly brothers and few faithful sisters. Though this is happening in many parts of the world (with very few exceptions), it may be more evident in UK and North America, New Zealand, and Australia. Some assemblies have lost their identity and have joined with other evangelical groups. Others have labeled themselves as independent churches and do not wish to be known as "assemblies." In most places, very few assemblies are newly formed[8].

One point worthy of notice is that assemblies have been closing in great numbers even during periods when there was also great growth in the movement. For example,

Tim Grass gives numbers of new assemblies being opened as well as (in brackets) assemblies disappearing in the years 1915 to 1944 in the United Kingdom[9]:

	England	Scotland	Wales	N. Ire.	Total
1915 – 24	180 (97)	73 (35)	23 (10)	27 (13)	303 (155)
1925 – 34	242 (174)	56 (68)	43 (10)	16 (7)	357 (259)
1935 – 44	126 (104)	26 (29)	10 (9)	12 (1)	174 (143)
Total	548 (375)	155 (132)	76 (29)	55 (21)	834 (557)

834 new assemblies opened in the years 1915 – 1944, but 557 assemblies also closed. Tim Grass gives the following figures from UK assemblies in the years 1945 to 2004:

	England	Scotland	Wales	N. Ireland	Total
1945 – 54	99 (66)	23 (31)	7 (4)	8 (4)	137 (105)
1955 – 64	101 (92)	14 (39)	7 (7)	1 (8)	123 (146)
1965 – 74	72 (82)	10 (38)	11 (4)	2 (2)	95 (126)
1975 – 84	31 (195)	10 (36)	4 (13)	8 (8)	53 (252)

1985 – 94	59 (116)	9 (24)	6 (15)	5 (3)	79 (158)
1995 – 04	25 (147)	0 (31)	1 (11)	5 (4)	31 (193)
Total	387 (698)	66 (199)	36 (54)	29 (29)	545 (980)

In the years from the Second World War to 2004, nearly 1000 assemblies closed in the United Kingdom. Since then, many more have disappeared.

Why should people who are not from the United Kingdom care about these facts? Because it was mostly missionaries from the United Kingdom or North America that originally planted Brethren assemblies in other countries. Even where God's work is going well in other parts of the world today, assemblies in these countries have similar spiritual DNA to Brethren churches from the UK and US, and so the same problems in British Brethren assemblies will be faced elsewhere sooner or later.

Later in this book, I will suggest there are four structural issues in Brethren assemblies which have led to the decline we are experiencing. But I will also argue that there are five factors which led to phenomenal growth in the past, and are still at work today. God can revive His work – even in Western countries. God does not need great numbers of people to work, nor is there any situation too hard or small for Him to do great things. We need to understand the principles that result in growth and strength, and at the same time rightly diagnose the weaknesses that cause decline. To use an unspiritual and overworked analogy, the question for us is this: how do we close the back door (stop people leaving) and how do we get more people in the front door (see new people saved and churches planted)? Or to use a medical analogy, what is making us so spiritually unwell, and what medicine do we need to take to recover?

Reasons for the Decline of Assemblies

In this book, I will argue that the reasons for the decline of Brethren assemblies are primarily spiritual, not societal, and the cure is spiritual too. That is, although there are factors at work in Western society which make spiritual growth difficult, these are not the real reasons for assembly decline. Here are five false diagnoses – five external, societal, factors that have affected assembly life:

1. After the Second World War, Western society saw major demographic changes. Inner-city slums were cleared, and large numbers of foreign migrants also displaced the original inhabitants in many inner-city areas. Increasing post-war educational opportunities also saw families moving to more affluent suburbs. This resulted in numbers of people in inner-city assemblies declining dramatically, so that many closed. With technological improvements in agriculture, less work in country areas meant young people moved away from home, again resulting in a decline in numbers of people in country assemblies.
2. The entertainment industry took off in the post-war period. We live in the show business age. The coming of television had a major impact on society, and

negatively affected assemblies in three ways. First, television killed off Sunday School work in much of the Western world. Instead of a free child-minding service, parents could sit their children down in front of the television on Sundays. As a result, thriving Sunday Schools dwindled down to a few children by 1980, diminishing evangelistic opportunities and contacts with society at large. As a result, many teachers were now out of a job and, because Christians become (and stay) healthy by actively serving God in sharing His Word, the end of effective Sunday School work also negatively impacted Christian growth in many peoples' lives. Thirdly, watching television proved increasingly attractive to Christians too. The average Western person spent approximately 3 hours per day watching television before the advent of the internet (and since then 'screen time' has only increased). Whereas believers in assemblies once had a reputation for spending their spare evenings studying the Bible, so that they were known as 'people of the Book', believers were now increasingly letting 'the world squeeze you into its mould' (Romans 12:2, *Phillips*).

3. Other post-war changes in society, particularly the sexual revolution, technological advances, increasing prosperity, and growing secularism, have also taken their toll on believers' lives. The Lord said, 'and because lawlessness will abound, the love of many will grow cold' (Matt. 24:12). With believers less focused on their spiritual life, the results of spiritual ill-health

are increasingly evident: materialism, family breakdown, and people abandoning the faith.
4. The charismatic movement drew off some Christians from assemblies. Offering 'something more' for those eager to see God at work, some believers fell for the claimed super-spirituality, the charismatic movement divided some assemblies, and some charismatic leaders came from assembly backgrounds.
5. Later, the American 'seeker-sensitive' model of church life also impacted assemblies. Even in the USA, while megachurches have led to the conversion of people, they have not increased the proportion of the population attending church. Most Christians attending megachurches are largely transfer growth (a.k.a. sheep-stealing) from smaller, struggling churches. Despite the rest of the Western world being nowhere near as religious as the USA, many churches elsewhere copied this model of church, drawing believers away from assemblies.

The reason why we cannot attribute the demise of the assemblies to these causes is because all other churches faced the same problems, but no other group of evangelical churches has suffered the same dramatic drop-off in numbers as the assemblies.

The following graph shows the annual growth or decline of various denominations in the UK in 2015-2020. Churches are coloured light grey if they are liberal in theology, medium grey if they are a mixture of liberal and evangelical (Baptists and Church of England, which are decreasing at over 2% per year!), black if they are evangelical (which includes charismatics), and white for the Roman Catholic church. The only group coloured black, i.e. evangelical, and yet in decline is the Open Brethren (seventh bar from the right)[10]. (Total UK church attendance is dropping at 10% per decade, so much of the growth on the right of the graph comes from the left).

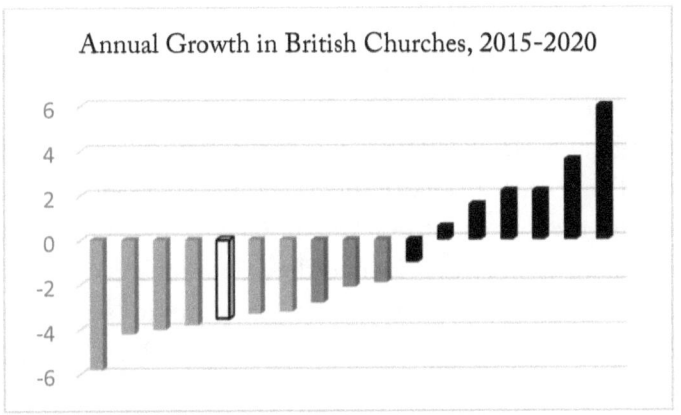

The Roman Catholic church tends to blame its decline on the breakdown of the traditional family as a result of the sexual revolution (see for example, *How the West Really Lost God*, by Mary Eberstadt). But, while true, this excuse ignores other important factors, like the fact that they do not preach the true gospel.

The second sort of churches in dramatic decline are liberal 'mainstream' churches, that is, those that have abandoned the faith and deny the great doctrines of the Christian gospel: the inspiration and inerrancy of Scripture, the deity of Christ, His substitutionary atoning death, His bodily resurrection, and justification by faith. Liberal churches nowadays use their pulpits to promote a social gospel, or maybe even the latest radical political, sexual, and environmental agendas. No one needs to go to church to hear about these topics – so people leave.

But why are Brethren assemblies also in dramatic decline? It is not because of doctrinal apostasy – like theologically liberal churches. The assemblies are still amongst the staunchest defenders of the great truths of God's Word, despite much weakness. Nor is family breakdown the main reason for assembly decline. So, why the great decline? Why are assemblies dying?

The Irish-Canadian evangelist Harold Paisley used to quote the words of Rachel in Gen. 30:1, 'Give me children, or else I die'. Here is the main problem – we are not seeing outsiders saved. If we were to see non-Christians converted, many of our problems would disappear. Much of this book is devoted to this issue, but there are also other reasons our churches are dying.

Before we start looking at these reasons, we need to ask, who are the Brethren, and why does their decline matter? In the following chapter I shall attempt to describe seven defining characteristics of the Brethren, and give a short history of the movement.

Chapter Two

WHO ARE THE BRETHREN?

The Brethren movement is the story of a dozen or so young men and how God used them to do remarkable things. This is not just ancient history – God can do the same again today. Here is their story, and seven principles they held (warning: a few long quotes follow):

1. Love for all who Belong to Christ

In 1826 in Ireland Edward Cronin, a recent convert from Roman Catholicism, moved to Dublin to study medicine. When he had earlier travelled to Dublin as a visitor, he made friends with evangelical Christians, and when he visited Dissenting churches (i.e. Protestant, non-Anglican churches) he was welcomed at the Lord's Supper. But he was also disturbed by the rivalry amongst Protestant sects. What an embarrassing sight all the divided denominations, who had the true gospel, made by comparison with the united front that Catholicism presented, despite its many errors. When he moved permanently to Dublin to study medicine, he was told that he must apply for special membership in one church. Cronin was reluctant to do this because if he became a member of one denomination he would be refused fellowship with Christian friends in other churches. He stated that 'the Church of God was one, and that all who believed were members of that one Body'. After being publicly denounced from the pulpit for this by one of the ministers, he started meeting together with Edward Wilson, Assistant Secretary of the Bible Society in Dublin. Soon after, John Nelson Darby, John Gifford Bellett, Francis Hutchinson, John Parnell, Anthony Norris Groves, and others joined them, to break bread as a demonstration of Christian unity.

Christian unity was the issue – the spark – that ignited the Brethren movement. The Victorian novelist George MacDonald put it as well as anyone else: 'Division has done more to hide Christ from the view of men, than all the infidelity that has ever been spoken'.

In 1828, J. N. Darby published what has been called 'the first Brethren tract' titled *Considerations on the Nature and Unity of the Church of Christ*. It began by quoting the words of our Lord Jesus on the night before His death from John 17:21, 'That they all may be one, as thou, Father, art in me, and I in thee, that they may be one in us, that the world may believe that thou hast sent me' (John 17:21). Darby not only lamented the sad state of disunity among true Christians, but he went further, rejecting the idea of denominations altogether, as their unity was based, not on the true oneness of the people of God, but on their differences from other believers. He saw the solution to the problem of Christian disunity not in a reformation of denominations (he considered his own, the Church of Ireland, to be beyond hope; many of the clergy were not born again, and it was a state church, i.e. wedded to the secular government and wielding political power). Nor did he argue for a union of denominations, for he argued that true unity is a unity of the Spirit. He wrote that any union of denominations would simply be a 'counterpart to Romish unity; we should have the life of the church and the power of the Word lost'. Instead, he argued that the outward symbol and instrument of unity is the partaking of the Lord's Supper (quoting 1 Cor. 10:17, "for we being many are one body, for we are all partakers of that one bread"). Therefore, he felt his only course of action was to be found in the words of Matthew 18:20, 'where two or three are gathered together in My name, there am I in the midst of them'. Accordingly, he started meeting together with a small number of other like-minded souls.

Anthony Norris Groves wrote in 1828:

> My full persuasion is, that inasmuch as any one glories either in being of the Church of England, Scotland, Baptist, Wesleyan, Independent, etc., his glory is in his shame, and that it is anti-Christian; for as the apostle said, 'Were any of them crucified for you?' The only legitimate ground of glorying is, that we are among the ransomed of the Lord by His grace. As *bodies* I know none of the sects and parties that wound and disfigure the body of Christ; as individuals I desire to love all who love Him[11].

Here are three other letters from Darby that show the importance of Christian unity to the early Brethren:

- 'I do trust that you will keep infinitely far from sectarianism. The great body of Christians who are accustomed to religion, are scarce capable of understanding anything else ... You are nobody, nothing, but Christians, and the moment you cease to be an available mount for communion for any consistent Christian, you will go to pieces or help the evil'[12].
- (Quoting from Romans 15:7): 'Whenever Christ has received a person, we should receive him. That false brethren may creep in unawares is possible. If the church is spiritual they will soon be made apparent; but as our table is the Lord's and not ours, we receive all the Lord has received'[13].
- Near the end of his life, Darby deals with the question of whether to receive a brother from another church who is known to be 'godly and sound in faith' but has not 'left some ecclesiastical system, nay, thinks Scripture favours an ordained ministry', and who is visiting a place where there is an assembly, and comes along: 'Is he to be shut out? If so, the degree of light is title to communion, and the unity of the body is denied by the assembly which refused him. The principle of meeting as members of Christ walking in godliness is given up, agreement with us is made the rule, and the Assembly becomes a sect with its members like any other. They meet on their principles, Baptist or other – you on yours, and if they do not belong to you formally as such, you do not let them in. The principle of the brethren's meetings is

gone, and another sect is made, say with more light, and that is all. It may give more trouble, require more care to treat every case on its merits, on the principle of the unity for all of Christ's brethren, than say "You do not belong to us; you cannot come". But the whole principle of meeting is gone. The path is not of God'[14].

The early Brethren not only believed in the One Body, the great truth of Ephesians, but practised it by receiving all those who were Christ's, that is, those who confessed faith in Christ and evidenced this by a godly life. They also refused to take any distinctive name to differentiate themselves from other Christians (the name 'the Brethren' was a nickname given to them by others). Unity in Christ was their basis of fellowship. Their motto was 'Christ, not a creed' and 'life, not light'.

Some today, misunderstanding the position of the early Brethren, argue that they allowed anyone to walk in and join them at the Lord's Supper (an 'open table'). But this was not the case. Consider the 'Tottenham Memorandum' of 1849, still mounted on the wall at Brook Street Chapel:

We find our centre of union with each other and with all saints, as **one in Him***, and our power of fellowship by the Holy Spirit. We therefore desire to receive to the Lord's table those whom he has received; time being allowed for confidence to be established in our minds that those whom we receive are indeed the Lord's, and opportunity afforded* *for inquiring into and clearing away any imputation or occasion of scandal in any so applying. We welcome to the table,* **on individual grounds**, *each saint, not because he or she is a member of this or that gathering or denomination of Christians nor because they are followers of any particular leader, but on such testimony as commends itself to us as being sufficient. We distinctly refuse to be parties to any exclusion of those who, we are satisfied, are believers, except on grounds personally applying to their individual faith and conduct.*

Despite the fact that the Brethren movement started as a stand for Christian unity, a different version of the history is sometimes told today. Some say that the early Brethren simply met 'to remember the Lord', or that God revealed important biblical truths about church gathering to them. However, all other Protestant churches already observed the Lord's Supper. Furthermore, while God indeed revealed important truths to these early Brethren, these truths came later, as a result of their continuing study of the Scriptures.

It must also be remembered that while unity in Christ was the initial basis of their fellowship, it is (paradoxically) true that Brethren assemblies also sprung up as a result of dissatisfaction with, a protest against, some of the evils in Christendom around them. In effect, the early Brethren had two principles of fellowship, love and truth.

Thus, for some who left the Anglican church to join the Brethren, like the evangelical clergymen Henry Borlase and James Harris, the problem with the Church of England was that it allowed many unsaved people to take the Lord's Supper but excluded true believers who did not belong to their communion. Ministers were required to conduct the burial services of ungodly people and had to assure the relatives that the deceased, who had lived a sinful life with no evidence of conversion, was now in heaven, simply because they were members of the Church of England. They were also required to baptise the infant children of ungodly people and pronounce them inheritors of the kingdom of God, even though they knew there was little likelihood that they would be any different from their parents.

Others left the non-conformist (i.e. non-Anglican) Protestant denominations because, although evangelical in doctrine, these churches were too narrow in their basis of fellowship, only receiving those who belonged to their sect and accepted their distinctive doctrines. The early Brethren felt this contradicted the teachings of the Lord Jesus on reception, where He said (speaking in a chapter about the local church), 'Whoever receives one little child like this in My name receives Me. But whoever causes one of these little ones who believe in Me to stumble, it would be better for him if a millstone were hung around his neck, and he were drowned in the depth of the sea' (Matt. 18:5-6, see also Mark 9:37, Luke 9:48). By receiving another believer, we receive Christ Himself. Paul teaches the same principle of reception in Romans 14:1 and 15:7.

Blair Neatby, in his history of the Brethren, put it like this: 'This twofold position was negatively expressed in their favourite dictum that the Church of England was too broad in its basis, and the dissenting churches too narrow'[15].

Darby withdrew from the Church of Ireland due to its politicisation, particularly the law by Archbishop Magee requiring Catholic converts to swear allegiance to the crown of England, which effectively killed off evangelism in Ireland. Darby viewed the true Church as a *spiritual* entity composed of all those belonging to Christ. He saw the church as a heavenly body united to its Head, not an earthly bureaucracy: we are 'seated together (with Christ) in the heavenly places in Christ' (Eph. 2:6).

Over time, Darby increasingly came to see that Christian unity involved not only love for all who belong to Christ, but also 'separation from evil'. He considered the different denominations – Roman Catholic, Anglican, and the dissenting churches – to be hopelessly ruined, and felt his only course of action was to 'come out and be separate'. But after some years, Darby felt he needed to separate from other 'brethren', too, over doctrinal disagreements. As a result, Darby first severed communion with Benjamin Newton (one of the leading brethren in Plymouth) over differing views on prophecy and church order, and then (when Newton was found teaching serious doctrinal error), Darby excommunicated all assemblies that received any believers from Plymouth, whether they held the error that Newton taught or not.

Darby's 'separation from evil' principle turned his gatherings which were originally 'an available mount for communion for any consistent Christian' into what his followers increasingly considered to be 'the only true church of God on earth'. Darby attempted to organise and co-ordinate the actions of a circle of assemblies under his control, and later Darby's Exclusive Brethren fragmented into multiple branches, separating over the slightest differences. By the 1950s, the main Exclusive branch had a 'centralized dictatorial leadership'[16] under James Taylor Jnr., which called for even more extreme forms of separation: all members in earthly professional associations (doctors, lawyers, etc.) were forced to give up their registrations in these professions. Marriages and families were broken up as Christian members were forced to separate from unsaved spouses and children. Even pets were banned. Separation was taken to an illogical and unscriptural extreme and destroyed the Exclusive Brethren as a force for God. As Darby himself had earlier prophesied, by abandoning the original position, his 'Exclusive Brethren' did indeed 'go to pieces [and] help the evil'.

Groves wrote to Darby as early as 1836, suggesting that Darby was 'returning to the city from whence you departed':

> I ever understood our principle of communion to be the possession of the common life ... these were our early thoughts, and are my most matured ones. The transition your little bodies have undergone, in no longer standing forth the witnesses for the glorious and simple truth, so much as standing forth witnesses against all that they judge error, have lowered them in my apprehension from heaven to earth ... And the

position which this occupying the seat of judgment will place you in will be this: the most narrow-minded and bigoted will rule, because his conscience cannot and will not give way ... It is into this position, dear Darby, I feel some little flocks are fast tending, if they have not already attained it[17].

The foundational principle of the Brethren movement was the unity of God's people based on biblical principles of Christian fellowship and reception. But they also distanced themselves from evil doctrine or practice. The Brethren movement was an attempt to honour these two great principles simultaneously. As their history showed, this is not always easy.

2. True Discipleship

In 1825, Anthony Norris Groves, a prosperous young dentist making a small fortune every year, wrote a little booklet titled, *Christian Devotedness*. Historian Tim Grass gives this summary of its contents:

> Groves called on Christians to dedicate themselves and their property to God, and to stop laying up treasure on earth, trusting instead to God's promises to provide for those who give up all for Him[19].

To his credit, Groves put his preaching into practice: selling his house, giving away his dental practice to a young relative, distributing his wealth to the poor and to gospel work. Then in 1829, after having been part of the first brethren assembly in Dublin, he gave up the comforts of life in Britain and went to Baghdad as a missionary, 'having trekked more than two thousand miles over desert, rocks and mountains'[20] with his wife and three young children. There he faced a war, a flood and then the plague, one after the other. As a result of these calamities, 60,000 out of Baghdad's population of 85,000 perished. To the plague, Groves also lost his wife Mary, and his little daughter. After all these disasters, he also had to endure fanatical Muslim opposition to the gospel. Rejected there, Groves went on to preach the gospel in India for 20 years.

Roy Coad, in his *History of the Brethren Movement*, titled a chapter, "The Call of Discipleship", and wrote:

> Of all the features that characterised the early leaders of the Brethren, the most attractive was the strength of their personal devotion to Christ. It was probably the strongest of the motives which moved them, as it was certainly entirely altruistic. Men may well question many of their practices and teachings, but none can deny the force of sacrificial lives of simplicity and true saintliness[18].

While the outward issue over which the early Brethren started meeting together was the unity of all true believers, a second, deeper characteristic was their total, 'all-out commitment to the Lord Jesus Christ'[21]. They took Christ's words to 'deny yourself, take up the cross and follow Me' (Matt. 16:24), to 'forsake all' (Luke 14:33), and to 'not lay up for yourselves treasure on earth' (Matt.

6:19) seriously. They considered that, in view of Christ's sacrifice, anything less than whole-hearted devotion to His cause was an inadequate response, and so they gave up everything for His sake.

John Nelson Darby was another one of the early Brethren who gave up everything for Christ. Darby was from an aristocratic family, the youngest son of Sir John Darby of Leap Castle, Ireland. Darby's uncle was an admiral who fought with Lord Nelson, the hero of the Battle of Trafalgar, hence Darby's middle name. After graduating with highest honours at Trinity College, Dublin (the main university in Ireland) he gave up his career as a barrister, much to his father's displeasure. He became a Church of Ireland clergyman, knowing no other way to serve God, and began ministry as an itinerant evangelist among the poor in rural parts of Ireland. Then he abandoned his ministerial position and association with the State Church to be a travelling evangelist and Bible teacher. Darby felt that 'since Christ had given all for him, therefore he owed all to Christ'[22].

John Vesey Parnell was the oldest son of Lord Congleton, and became a Christian at Edinburgh University after reading Paul's letter to the Romans. His father was so unhappy to hear that his son had become an evangelical Christian that, to cure his religious mania, he bought him an army posting. But instead of going into the army, Parnell began to preach on the streets, receiving in return insults and buckets of water over his head. Soon after this, he read Groves' booklet *Christian Devotedness* and dedicated his life entirely to God's work. Parnell was instrumental in the formation of the first assembly in Dublin, as a result of his desire to have fellowship with all other genuine Christians. He too went with Groves to Baghdad as a missionary, and later in life, as Lord Congleton, despite a seat in the House of Lords, continued to live by the principles of *Christian Devotedness*. His living arrangements were described as 'somewhat primitive' in a cheap rented house, with a plain wooden table and chairs, and no carpets on the floor. He then later sold almost all of his property, and devoted half of his income as a peer of the realm to God's service.

George Müller described the effect of reading Groves' booklet *Christian Devotedness* as a 'second conversion'. His reaction was 'an entire and full surrender of heart. I gave myself fully to the Lord. Honour, pleasure, money, my physical powers, my mental powers, all was laid down at the feet of Jesus, and I became a great lover of the word of God'.

Müller went on to become the most famous example of someone 'living by faith', as it has been called. After abandoning his salary as a clergyman, Müller not only lived by faith himself, but also established an orphanage in Bristol where he supported thousands of orphans throughout the 19th century, without making any appeal for funds, instead depending on God in prayer to supply the many needs of his expanding work. His autobiography, not just telling the story of the way that God supported him and his orphans but also describing the way that he had grown in maturity as a Christian, was perhaps the most influential of all the early Brethren writings.

Some today mock the idea of 'living by faith' as a clever scheme by which missionaries can get others to financially support them instead of working at an honest trade for their own support. What they fail to mention is that what primarily motivated these early brethren was a willingness to take Christ's words literally, and following Christ's example, to first 'sell all that you have', give away all their possessions, live simply, and without salary or any earthly support, venture their lives upon their faith that the Lord would supply their needs.

Historian Robert Dann wrote about the Brethren missionaries who went out following Anthony Norris Groves' example of living by faith:

> Thousands did. Following the example of Norris and Mary Groves they have set out in simple dependence on the living God to proclaim the story of a Saviour's love to the ends of the earth. They have gone cheerfully, without appeals for money, without contract or salary, without the protection of weapons or law, with the support of trustees, patrons or governments. They are sons, daughters, heirs of Norris Groves, and like him they have proof of the faithfulness of God. They too can say, "We have always had more than enough"[23].

Other names of early Brethren could be added to the list of those who gave up all to follow Christ:

- Francis Hutchinson, one of the original members of the first assembly in Dublin, was the son and heir of a Baronet, Rev. Sir Samuel Synge, who was also Archdeacon of Killala. Francis Hutchinson died in his early 30s before he inherited the title of Baronet himself, but it was in his house that the first assembly in Dublin met. Although we are not told what his father the Baronet and Archdeacon thought of such proceedings, he doubtless suffered the contempt of some others in high society circles.
- Captain Wellesley, son of Baron Cowley and nephew of the Duke of Wellington (Arthur Wellesley, who defeated Napoleon at Waterloo and was twice British Prime Minister), gave up his high society position to travel extensively in the British Isles preaching the gospel and teaching God's Word,
- Captain Percy Hall, whose father had been Regius Professor of Divinity (i.e. theology) and Dean of Christ Church (i.e. the cathedral) in Oxford, and who himself was a captain in the Royal Navy, likewise gave up his military career and commenced preaching the gospel, resulting in great blessing in Hereford.
- Robert Cleaver Chapman resigned his career as a solicitor, gave away his possessions and engaged in full-time Christian ministry, resulting in a great work of God in the town of Barnstaple.
- Henry Soltau was educated at Cambridge University, then became a barrister and a man of the world, enjoying its pleasures. When he was converted upon the death of his mother, he turned his back on it all,

and from then on, 'to live was Christ'. He gave up his legal career to devote himself to teaching the Bible and preaching the gospel.

Such devotion to Christ was not just seen among the leaders of the Brethren. The historian Andrew Miller writes, 'It was no uncommon thing at this time to find valuable jewelry in the collection boxes, which was soon turned into money, and given to the deacons for the poor'.

3. The Supreme Authority of Scripture

Henry Groves, Lord Congleton's biographer, wrote that three truths were of special importance to the early Brethren: '1st. The oneness of the Church of God, involving a fellowship large enough to embrace all saints, and narrow enough to exclude the world. 2nd. The completeness and sufficiency of the written Word in all matters of faith, and pre-eminently in things affecting our Church life and walk. 3rd. The speedy pre-millennial advent of the Lord Jesus'[24]. Professor Rendle-Short in his book, *The Principles of Christians called Open Brethren*, titled his second chapter, "The Divine Authority of the Bible". The Brethren were, above all, people of the Book.

Here are two examples of how the authority of Scripture worked out in real life in the experience of George Müller. First, here is Müller's discovery of the Bible's true place in the Christian's life:

> I fell into the snare into which so many young believers fall – the reading of religious books in preference to

the Scriptures. I could no longer read French and German novels as I had formerly done to feed my carnal mind; but still I did not put in the place of those books the best of all books. I read tracts, missionary papers, sermons, and biographies of godly persons. The last kind of books I found more profitable than the others, and had they been well selected, or had I not read too much of them, or had any of them served to endear the Scriptures to me, they might have done me much good. I had never been in the habit of reading the Holy Scriptures.

Now the scriptural way of reasoning would have been: God Himself has condescended to become an author, and I am ignorant about that precious Book, which His Holy Spirit has caused to be written by His servants, and it contains that which I ought to know to lead me to true happiness; therefore I ought to read this precious Book most earnestly, most prayerfully, and with much meditation; and in this I ought to continue all the days of my life ... But instead of acting thus, for the first four years of my divine life, I preferred the works of uninspired men to the oracles of the living God. In consequence I remained a baby, both in knowledge and in grace.

A few days after my arrival in Teignmouth, Devon, the chapel called Ebenezer, was re-opened, and I attended the opening. I was much impressed by one of those who preached on the occasion. For though I did not like all he said, yet I saw a gravity and solemnity in him different from the rest. After he preached I had a great desire to know more of him; and being invited by two brethren of Exmouth, in whose house he was staying, to spend some time with them, I had an opportunity of living ten days with him under the same roof. Through this brother the Lord bestowed a great blessing on me, for which I shall have cause to thank Him throughout eternity.

One of the points which God then began to show me was that the Word of God alone is our standard of judgment in spiritual things; that it can be explained only by the Holy Spirit; and that in our day, as well as in former times, He is the teacher of His people. The office of the Holy Spirit I had not experimentally understood before that time.

The Holy Spirit alone can teach us about our state by nature, show us the need of the Saviour, enable us to believe in Christ, explain to us the Scriptures, and help us in our preaching. It was my beginning to understand this latter point in particular, which had a great effect on me; for the Lord enabled me to put it to the test of experience, by laying aside commentaries, and almost every other book, and simply reading the Word of God and studying it.

The result of this was that the first evening I shut myself into my room to give myself to prayer and meditation over the Scriptures, I learned more in a few hours that I had done during a period of several months previously. But the particular difference was that I received real strength for my soul in doing so.

Secondly, here is Müller on the question of baptism:

> About the beginning of April (1830) I went to preach at Sidmouth. While I was staying there, three sisters in the Lord had, in my presence, a conversation about baptism. One of them had been baptized after she had believed. After they had conversed a little on the subject, I was asked to give my opinion concerning it. I replied, 'I do not think I need to be baptized again'.
>
> I was then asked by the sister who had been baptized, 'But have you been baptized?'
>
> I answered, 'Yes, when I was a child'.
>
> She then replied, 'Have you ever read the Scriptures, and prayed with reference to this subject?'
>
> I answered, 'No'.
>
> She then replied, 'I beg you never to speak any more about it until you have done so'.
>
> The Lord showed me the importance of this remark. For, while at that very time I was exhorting everyone to receive nothing which could not be proved by the Word of God, I had repeatedly spoken against believers' baptism, without having ever earnestly examined the Scriptures, or prayed concerning it. Now I determined, if God would help me, to examine that subject also, and if infant baptism were found to be scriptural, I would earnestly defend it; and if believers' baptism were right, I would as strenuously defend that, and be baptized.
>
> As soon as I had time, I set about examining the subject. The mode I adopted was as follows: I

repeatedly asked God to teach me concerning it, and I read the New Testament from the beginning with particular reference to this point. But now, when I earnestly set about the matter, a number of objections presented themselves to my mind.

First, since many holy and enlightened men have been divided in opinion concerning this point, does this not prove that it is not to be expected we should come to a satisfactory conclusion about this question in the present imperfect state of the Church? This question was thus removed: if this ordinance is revealed in the Bible, why may I not know it, as the Holy Spirit is the teacher in the Church of Christ now as well as formerly?

Second, there have been but few of my friends baptized, and the greater part of them are opposed to believers' baptism, and they will turn their backs on me. Answer: though all men should forsake me, if the Lord Jesus takes me up, I shall be happy.

Third, you will be sure to lose half of your income if you are baptized. Answer: as long as I desire to be faithful to the Lord, He will not suffer me to want.

Fourth, people will call me a Baptist, and you will be reckoned among that body, and you cannot approve of all that is going on among them. Answer: it does not follow that I must in all points go along with all those who hold believers' baptism, although I should be baptized.

Fifth, you have been preaching for some years, and you will thus publicly have to confess that you have been in error, should you come to the conclusion that believers' baptism is right. Answer: it is much better to confess that I have been in error than to continue in it.

Sixth, even if believers' baptism should be right, yet it is now too late to attend to it, as you ought to have been baptized immediately on believing. Answer: it is better to fulfil a commandment of the Lord Jesus ever so late, than to continue in the neglect of it.

It had pleased God to bring my mind into such a state that I was willing to carry out in my life whatever I should find in the Scriptures concerning this ordinance, either one way or the other. I could say, 'I will do His will', and it was on that account that I believe that I soon saw which doctrine was of God, whether infant baptism or believers' baptism.

As soon as I was brought into this state of heart, I saw from the Scriptures that believers only are the proper subjects for baptism, and that immersion is the only true scriptural mode in which it ought to be attended to. The passage which particularly convinced me of the former is Acts 8:36-8, and of the latter, Romans 6:3-5.

Some time after, I was baptized. I had much peace in doing so, and never have I for one single moment regretted it.

Müller also went on to make this important point:

My conviction now is that of all revealed truths not one is more clearly revealed in the Scriptures, and that the subject has only become obscured by men not having been willing to take the *Scriptures alone* to decide the point.

The early Brethren treated the Bible as the very Word of God. They applied the Lord's own test, 'What does the Scripture say?' (Luke 10:26, Rom. 4:13, Gal. 4:30), to decide any question. Rather than taking a post-modern, pick-and-choose approach, they tried to obey all that the Scripture teaches (Ps. 119:128, Matt. 4:4, 28:20) rejecting human tradition, reasoning, experience, or culture. C. H. Mackintosh stated their position:

> Men must either deny that the Bible is the Word of God, or admit its sufficiency and supremacy in all ages. . . . Neither tradition nor expediency will do for the servant of Christ. The all-important inquiry is, "What saith the Scriptures." This settles everything. From the decision of the Word of God there must be no appeal. When God speaks man must bow. It is not by any means a question of obstinate adherence to a man's own notions. Quite the opposite. It is a reverent adherence to the Word of God. Let the reader distinctly mark this. It often happens that, when one is determined, through grace, to abide by Scripture, he will be pronounced dogmatic, intolerant, and imperious; and, no doubt, one has to watch over his temper, spirit, and style, even when seeking to abide by the Word of God. But, be it well remembered, that obedience to Christ's commandments is the very

opposite of imperiousness, dogmatism, and intolerance. It is not a little strange that when a man tamely consents to place his conscience in the keeping of his fellow, and to bow down his understanding to the opinions of men, he is considered meek, modest, and liberal; but let him reverently bow to the authority of the Holy Scripture, and he will be looked upon as self-confident, dogmatic, and narrow-minded. Be it so. The time is rapidly approaching when obedience shall be called by its right name, and meet its recognition and reward[25].

Like all other Christians, the Brethren have not perfectly obeyed or understood Scripture. Over time, some added their own man-made rules and traditions to God's Word, while others have quietly ignored or disobeyed things that God has commanded. But here we have another foundational characteristic of the Brethren: they took the Bible as their final and only infallible authority and tried to put it into practice.

4. Devotion to Christ

Here we come to the ultimate foundation of the Brethren. Rendle-Short listed the Deity of Christ as the first of *The Principles of Christians called Open Brethren.*

The early Brethren all came to realise that salvation is through personal faith in Christ and His finished work – not good works, or birth, or church membership. All the other principles of the Brethren merely draw out the implications of this. It is the Son of God who tells us that the Scriptures are 'the Word of God' (Mark 7:13) 'which cannot be broken' (John 10:35), so Scripture is inspired and inerrant. It is because of Christ's own call that Christians 'deny themselves, take up the cross and follow Him'. Faith in Christ was their principle of unity and fellowship. 'We do not preach ourselves but Christ Jesus the Lord' (2 Cor. 4:5) was their missionary motto.

Probably the most noticable thing about a Brethren assembly today is its worship of Christ. This is seen in a traditional Brethren assembly at the Lord's Supper, which is largely given to remembrance of Christ. Love for Christ is also seen in the distinctive hymns of the Brethren. I still remember, as a boy, being powerfully impacted by the words of the hymn at the breaking of bread:

> How didst Thou humble Thyself to be taken,
> Led by Thy creatures and nailed to the cross?
> Hated of men and of God, too, forsaken,
> Shunning not darkness, the curse and the loss.
> (Henry d'Arcy Champney)

We could fill pages with the words of hymns that breathe love and devotion to Christ:

> Glory to Thee; Thou Son of God most High,
> all praise to Thee!
> Glory to Thee, enthroned above the sky,
> who died for me;
> high on Thy throne, Thine ear, Lord Jesus bend
> as grateful hearts now to Thyself ascend.

> Thorns wreathed Thy brow when hanging on the tree,
> Man's cruelty!
> Why lavish love like this, O Lord, on me!
> Thou lovest me!
> Would that my soul could understand its length,
> Its breadth, depth, height, and everlasting strength!
> (Edward C. Quine)

Not all Brethren hymns are distinctive. I still remember being moved to tears as a teenager as I sang the words of the third verse of one of the most popular of all English hymns, *How Great Thou Art*, composed by the 20th century Brethren missionary Stuart Hine:

> And when I think, that God His Son not sparing,
> Sent Him to die, I scarce can take it in,
> That on the cross, my burden gladly bearing,
> He bled and died, to take away my sin.

Christ must have the pre-eminent place.

5. Church Practices

The fifth defining characteristic of the 'brethren' was the adoption of distinctive church practices. While the Reformation applied the principle of *Sola Scriptura* (Scripture alone) to the doctrine of salvation, rejecting medieval traditions of the Roman Catholic church about salvation, the Brethren simply took this principle to its logical conclusion, and rejected Protestant traditions concerning Church government and practice.

When the first assembly met together to break bread in Dublin, they had very undeveloped views on church life. At the beginning, they left the order of service up to the man in whose house they were meeting. But as the small group of Christians continued studying Scripture, they came to realise that (in Groves' words) 'we should come together in all simplicity as disciples, not waiting on any pulpit or ministry, but trusting that the Lord would edify us together by ministering as He pleased and saw good from the midst of ourselves'.

Groves' own experience doubtless played a part in coming to this view. Groves had visited Dublin as a theology student, because he hoped to become a missionary, which at that time required ordination in the Church of England. This was because the Church of England forbad anyone apart from an ordained clergyman officiating at the Lord's Supper on the mission field. If Groves went out as a missionary and saw people converted, he would therefore not be able to gather them together in a church without being ordained. But, after much heart-searching and Bible study, Groves came to the conclusion that 'ordination of any kind to preach the gospel is no requirement of Scripture'. To preach the gospel was the right and obligation of every Christian. Once Groves saw that he did not need to be an ordained clergyman to preach the gospel, it was not long before he came to question where he had got the idea that a clergyman was required to officiate at the breaking of bread. He searched the New Testament in vain for any such office or ordination. Groves went out as a missionary convinced that (in the words of a later Brethren poet):

> Christ, the Son of God, hath sent me
> Through the midnight lands;
> Mine the mighty ordination
> Of the piercéd Hands[26].

Edward Cronin described the process as 'a growing feeling of opposition to one-man ministry'. Having been publicly denounced by a clergyman for failing to apply for special membership in one of the denominations, it is perhaps understandable that Cronin should not have much faith in Protestant clergymen. If an ordained minister was blind to the truth of the One Body, which even a new convert from Catholicism could see, then Cronin could hardly be forgiven for wondering what other Protestant church traditions were unbiblical.

Darby came to this realisation in a different way. As a clergyman himself, Darby saw some of the inconsistencies involved. In his letter to Professor Tholuck about the Brethren, Darby wrote:

> If the apostle Paul were to come here now, he would not, according to the established system [i.e. Church of England], be even allowed to preach, not being legally ordained; but if a worker of Satan, who, by his doctrine, denied the Saviour, came here, he could freely preach, and my Christian friend [a local

clergyman] would be obliged to consider him as a fellow-labourer; whereas he would be unable to recognize the most powerful instrument of the Spirit of God, however much blessed in the work of leading multitudes of souls to the Lord, if he has not been ordained according to the system. All this, said I to myself, is false. This is not mere abuse, such as may be found everywhere; it is the principle of the system that is at fault. Ministry is of the Spirit. There are some amongst the clergy who are ministers by the Spirit, but the system is founded on an opposite principle; consequently it seemed impossible to remain in it any longer' (*Letter to Professor Tholuck*, c.1857-59)

Darby's second tract was entitled, "The Notion of a Clergyman Dispensationally the Sin against the Holy Spirit". In it he wrote,

If the notion of a Clergyman has had the effect of the substitution of anything which is of man, ... in the place and prerogative of that blessed Spirit exercising the vicarship of Christ in the world ... the effect of this system ... is to deprive them [i.e. God's people] of the opportunity to stir up, or bar the exercise of, whatever gifts God may have made them partakers of[27].

Having done away with any horizontal divisions between Christians (denominationalism), the Brethren realized that the New Testament does not teach a vertical division of believers into clergy and laity (clericalism).

ASSEMBLY AUTOPSY

The main weekly Brethren meeting, centred around the breaking of bread, seems very strange to many Christians today. There is no minister up the front leading the service. There is no liturgy or set prayers read off a sheet. There is not even a formal order of service. Instead, there is freedom and opportunity for any of the brothers to rise and participate, sharing from the Scriptures, or leading in prayer, or suggesting a hymn to sing. Why did the early Brethren have church services like this? The answer is that they went back to the Bible and tried to follow what it taught about church gatherings.

Historian Robert Dann describes the meetings of the early Brethren:

> Their meetings were deliberately informal, like those described in the New Testament: "When you meet for worship, one person has a hymn, another a teaching, another a revelation from God ... All of you may proclaim God's message, one by one, so that everyone will learn and be encouraged" [1 Cor. 14:26,31]. Indeed, they found, as in the days of the apostles, that "the Spirit's presence is shown in some way in each person for the good of all'" [1 Cor. 12:7][28].

Most of the early leaders of the brethren (Darby, Groves, Müller, Craik, Chapman) were either clergymen or, in the case of Groves, studying to become one. But they came to realize that the New Testament does not describe any such office of one man who ministers the sacraments, preaches the Word, and leads or presides over their meetings. This is all contrary to the New Testament picture of free exercise of ministry in the church by those gifted for it by the Holy Spirit.

Not only did the early Brethren repudiate the clerical system as unscriptural, they also refused to take any clerical titles. God is the only person in Scripture described as 'reverend', while Christ forbad His disciples calling any man 'father' (Matt. 23:9). There is no such thing in the Bible as the 'senior pastor', unless we refer to Christ Himself, who is the chief Shepherd (1 Pet. 5:4).

Hence, they were known simply as brother X, (or, 'brethren' in the plural). This was soon used in mockery against them. Thus, Charles Dickens had an article in his newspaper titled, "Brother George Müller and His Orphan Work" which, by repeatedly calling him 'Brother Müller'[29], ridiculed him for a pretended humility.

Alongside the freedom to participate in ministry, the early Brethren also came to realise that church government is clearly taught in the New Testament. Thus, Müller and Craik, labouring together in Bristol, not only refused to be called 'Pastor', but in 1839 set aside two weeks of retreat, prayer and study to consider the question of church government and practices, and concluded from scripture that:

1. plural elders govern the church (Acts 14:23, 20:17, 1 Peter 5:1), being gifted and appointed by the Holy Spirit (Acts 20:28), confirmed by the possession of the required qualifications (1 Tim. 3:2-7, Tit. 1:6-9) and by blessing upon their labours (1 Cor. 9:2), and

acknowledged and submitted to in the Lord by the saints (1 Thess. 5:12-13, Heb. 13:7, 17).

2. the congregation has rights too: settling matters of discipline in the presence of the assembled church (Matt. 18:17, 1 Cor. 5:4-5), receiving all who make a credible profession of faith (Rom. 15:7), and opportunity for the free exercise of gifts of teaching or exhortation at the Lord's Supper as well as communion in prayer and praise (Rom. 12:4-8, Eph. 4:11-16). They wrote, 'though the meeting should not normally be in the hands of a single man, those who have gifts of teaching or exhortation should feel their responsibility to edify the church'[30].

Thus, the early brethren adopted a biblically-balanced blend of presbyterian (i.e. elder-led) government and congregational participation in the life of the church. Elders were to lead but members of the congregation also had important roles to play in the church.

Rendle-Short wrote:

> It is not right to regard the character of our worship as a matter of no importance. After laying down clear regulations for the conduct of the open meeting, Paul concludes with these striking words: "If any man thinketh himself to be a prophet, or spiritual, let him take knowledge of the things that I write unto you, that they are the commandments of the Lord. But if any man is ignorant, let him be ignorant." [1 Cor. 14:37]. If we read these words in their context, their

force is very apparent. The argument which a serious-minded man, who acknowledges the authority of the apostolic example, is most likely to employ against the open meeting is that the day of miraculous gifts is over, and that we cannot expect the Holy Spirit to guide a meeting now as He used to during the first century. No doubt the gifts of healing and of speaking with tongues have passed away. The special gift of inspiration which led Paul and others to write their Epistles has also passed away. But the Holy Spirit has not passed away. He abides with us for ever (John 14. 16); not only with the ordained minister, but with every believer (Rom. 8. 9). It is one of His functions to take of the deep things of God, and to reveal them to us. He spoke at Corinth not only through Apostles but also through obscure slaves. If He cannot speak to-day through the open meeting, which was His own original appointment, if all His ministrations were concluded in the first century, then we must believe that even John Wesley, C. H. Spurgeon, and D. L. Moody preached without His assistance. The open meeting shifts the responsibility of following the Spirit's leading from the minister to all the believers present, and a solemn but blessed responsibility it is.

6. Missionary and Gospel work

The Brethren movement was from the very outset a missionary movement. Anthony Norris Groves left for Baghdad in 1829, while two others of the original Dublin assembly, Cronin and Parnell (Lord Congleton), left to join him in 1830.

In fact, virtually all of the early Brethren were missionaries in some sense:

- George Müller came to England from Germany as a missionary to Jews.
- J. N. Darby travelled in Europe in the 1830s and 40s, particularly in Switzerland and France, where he established assemblies.
- R. C. Chapman, although based in Barnstaple, made three missionary visits to Spain before it was legal to distribute Bibles or preach the gospel.

Despite the current decline among assemblies in the western world, it is in its missionary emphasis that we see some of the most notable evidence that the Holy Spirit was at work in the Brethren movement. Even in 2004, Robert Dann could write, 'At the present time, a total of 380 missionaries are associated with Echoes of Service [the largest UK Brethren missionary reporting agency], a larger body of British workers than any Anglican, Baptist or other denominational mission in the UK'[31].

Newton and Chan wrote, 'In time, missionary endeavours out of Brethren churches became proverbial and up to one percent of members of Brethren churches volunteered for missionary work'[32]. Newton elsewhere argued that no other group (with the exception of the Moravians in the 1700s) had given mission the priority which the early Brethren did[33].

Anne Arnott, writing of the Brethren in the early

twentieth century, said, 'They were undoubtedly seen at their best on the mission field. Determined, intrepid, dedicated, they ventured into many lands, often pioneering where none had been before ... The large number who went overseas was higher than that of almost any other Christian group or denomination in proportion to their membership'[34].

One of the great missionary pioneers among the Brethren was Frederick Stanley Arnot (no relation to Anne Arnott!). He left Scotland for central Africa at the age of 23 in 1881 without the backing of any missionary society, looking to God for support. Arnot travelled on foot from the east coast of Africa to the west coast, opening up central Africa for missionary work. Sir Ralph Williams (who met him at Victoria Falls) described Arnot as a 'remarkable man ... [living] a life of great hardship ... with one desire, and that was to do God service ... I have honoured him ever since as being as near his Master as anyone I ever saw' (*How I Became Governor*).

Arnot went to Africa in the years not long after David Livingstone, before modern medicine or civilisation had arrived, knowing full well the dangers that such missionary work involved. He trekked into the interior in 1886 to visit the kingdom of the fearsome chief Msidi of Garenganze, whose compound was decorated with the skulls of his victims. There Arnot built a mission house. After a visit to England where he was honoured for his geographical explorations, he returned to Africa in 1889 with a large number of recruits for the mission field. But within a number of months, three of the party had died.

In 1914, Arnot travelled up the Zambesi river from Victoria Falls with two new missionary recruits, George Suckling and Thomas Lambert Rogers. Arnot was returning to a mission house he had earlier built near the junction of the Zambesi and Kabompo rivers. There Arnot's spleen ruptured, and he went to South Africa, where he died a few months later at the age of 56. Within two years Lambert Rogers had also died. George Suckling stayed on alone to set up a printing press, a school and, later, a leprosy mission and hospital at 'Chitokoloki', whose work continues today.

Many others followed in Arnot's footsteps, and stories like his could be repeated many times over. My grandfather's brother, T. Ernest Wilson, left Ireland in 1923 as a missionary at the age of 21 to evangelise unreached tribes in the north of Angola. He spent nearly 40 years in that country, living for years as the only white man within many miles. Today, the Brethren are the 'established church' of central Africa, with over 5000 assemblies through Angola, Congo, and Zambia.

Back in Britain, with other denominations abandoning the faith for liberal theology, it was said that the Brethren kept the flame of gospel outreach alight between the two world wars, not only preaching Christ in large 'tent cathedrals' in major cities, and in innumerable local gospel campaigns, but also by being involved in the growing work of evangelising university students through Christian unions.

Before that, in 1859, in the greatest revival ever seen in Britain, many prominent evangelists were Brethren, and the Brethren grew exponentially from it.

7. Doctrinal Distinctives

The Brethren have very few doctrinal peculiarities. Starting with the principle of Scripture as the final and only infallible authority, the Brethren have always been staunch defenders of orthodox, biblical Christianity. This is seen even in the most serious doctrinal dispute in Brethren history: the Benjamin Wills Newton affair that sparked the split between the Open and Exclusive Brethren in 1848. Newton was one of the most accomplished teachers and early leaders of the Brethren, but he suggested some erroneous ideas on the human nature of Christ, arguing that because of His birth, Christ's human nature shared in some of the consequences of the fall, including mortality, human guilt, and Israel's guilt. These views were publicly condemned by Darby, and Newton was forced to publish a retraction, confessing his errors. The whole affair shows the great care taken to safeguard the truths concerning the person and work of the Lord Jesus Christ.

The Brethren developed distinctive doctrinal views in one area: prophecy. Blair Neatby, the early historian of the Brethren movement, argued that 'Brethrenism is the child of the study of unfulfilled prophecy, and of the expectation of the immediate return of the Saviour'[35]. In Neatby's opinion, this occurred because of the desire of the Brethren to start from Scripture alone[36]. They simply took the Reformation principle of reading Scripture in its plain sense, employing a grammatical-historical method (and avoiding fanciful spiritualising), and extended it to the study of what the Bible says about future events.

Interest in Bible prophecy was increasing in the 1820s, following the French Revolution and Napoleonic Wars (1779-1815). The political upheavals in Europe made it difficult for evangelical Christians to continue holding to post-millennialism, the optimistic belief that everything in the world was getting better, and that eventually the whole world would be Christianized. Both in society and in the established Church, things were getting worse.

From 1826-30, annual conferences on future events were held at Albury, Surrey, attended by clergy from many places in Britain. Then in the 1830s, Lady Powerscourt arranged an annual week of meetings for the study of prophecy at her castle outside Dublin. Six of the early leaders of the Brethren took part in the Powerscourt conferences: Darby, J. G. Bellett, Capt. Percy Hall, B. W. Newton, George Müller and Henry Craik.

This is not the place to go into a full-blown discussion of future events. However, there were three major puzzles that the early Brethren wrestled with. Firstly, by reading Scripture in its ordinary, plain sense, the early Brethren quickly came to believe that there must be a literal millennium in the future after Christ's return. Francis Hutchinson, one of the original members of the Dublin assembly, engaged in a debate in the public press in 1830, arguing against post-millennialism.

A second question the early Brethren wrestled with was the future of the Jewish nation. Darby held (initially from Isaiah 32, and then from many other passages) that the Jewish nation's future is distinct from the church, and that there must be a future Jewish restoration to their land, and conversion to Christ.

Darby was also convinced by 2 Thessalonians 2 that there must be a future period of time before the return of Christ which is entirely different in character to the present church age, yet before the millennium. In this period, for example, God sends a strong delusion upon unbelievers so they should believe the lie (2 Thess. 2:11) – but no Christian believes God is doing this at present. This future period is before the millennium, but characterised by conditions diametrically opposed to the present time, so how can it be part of the church age?

A third puzzle involved the apparent contradiction Scripture presents between verses teaching that Christ's coming is imminent (about 50 New Testament verses suggest this) and, on the other hand, the Bible's teaching that certain clearly identifiable events (particularly the terrible events of the Great Tribulation) must precede the return of Christ. How can Christ's coming be a surprise – like a thief in the night – if there are devastating and unmistakable signs that occur immediately before it?

Darby's solution to this problem involved positing two stages to the Lord's coming: a rapture of the church (1 Thess. 4:13-17) before the tribulation period, followed by the return of Christ at the end of the tribulation. Other early Brethren (Newton, Müller and Craik) rejected Darby's view and preferred a post-tribulation rapture.

Darby's pretribulation rapture neatly solved at a stroke all three problems: Israel's distinct future, the fact that the

Bible teaches a period of time before the millennium with conditions that are the exact opposite of those occurring today, and how Christ's coming could be a surprise and yet preceded by unmistakable signs. Even George Müller apparently came to accept a pre-tribulation rapture in his later years[37]. Darby's teachings on prophecy are now the most popular view among evangelicals, at least in the USA, and probably elsewhere too[38].

One practical consequence of a distinction between Israel and the Church concerns whether Christians are under the Law. Should Christians keep Sabbath, tithe, have a clerical priesthood, take up the sword (like Israel's heroes) or eat shellfish and ham? Calvin argued that Christians are under the moral (but not the civil or ceremonial) law. The early Brethren taught that we are not under the law as a rule of life (Rom. 6:14-15, 7:4-7, 1 Cor. 9:19-20, Gal. 5:18, 1 Tim. 1:8-9 – note: these verses deal with moral life). The Christian is not a disciple of Moses but is under the law of Christ (Gal. 6:2, 1 Cor. 9:20), and obeys His teachings. Nor is this antinomianism (a lawless licence to indulge in sin). Christ sets for us a higher standard than Moses (see Matthew 5).

Ironside wrote, 'if "Brethren" are heretics because they teach that *Christ*, not the law of Moses, is the rule of life, they are in excellent company ... We are not under law (Rom. 6:14). We are neither saved by the law, nor under it, as a rule of life; we are not lawless, but "under law (enlawed) to Christ" [1 Cor. 9:19-20]. We stand firmly by the apostle Paul when he declares, "I through the law died unto the law that I might live to God" (Gal. 2:19). Is

Christ himself a lower standard than the law given at Sinai? Or is the latter needed to complete the former? Surely no intelligent believer would so speak. This is not antinomianism, but its very opposite. It is subjection to Christ as Lord of the New Dispensation and Mediator of the New Covenant'[39].

C. H. Mackintosh wrote, 'The law is not the rule of the believer's life ... Christ is our rule of life ... As to the believer's rule of life, the apostle does not say, To me to live is the law; but, "To me to live is Christ" (Phil. 1:21). Christ is our rule, our model, our touchstone, our all' (*The Sabbath, the Law, and Christian Ministry*).

Conclusion

The early Brethren were Christians characterized by faith, love, hope, zeal, devotion to Christ, radical obedience to God's Word, and missionary daring. This leaves us with two questions. First, with such good principles, how it is possible that the Brethren today should be in such serious decline? Second, is there any hope of recovery?

Chapter Three

HOW RECOVERY BEGINS

In the years 1857-1859, there was a remarkable work of God in Northern Ireland. James McQuilkin, a young Presbyterian who had recently been converted, was encouraged to do something for God, so he started a village Sunday School. Then he started a prayer meeting with three of his friends. For a while nothing seemed to happen. Then, after several months one man was saved, then a month later a Sunday School student came to Christ. Then, three months later, two people who had been specially prayed for professed faith in Christ. As Christians heard of people being converted the regular church prayer meetings started to get packed, and new prayer meetings sprung up. The number of converts grew and multiplied in this little country area, and over a period of 18 months about two hundred people were saved. This revival started to change the district: two of the local pubs closed when their owners were converted, a third was closed for lack of business, and the six pubs that remained open sold less than was formerly sold by one of them.

Then the work started spreading, as prayer meetings started in other places. Huge crowds gathered in the open air in the main country towns to listen to the gospel (often preached by new converts telling how they got saved) and when the preaching finished, people would fall down on their knees crying out to God for mercy. Every single night the churches were packed, and clergymen were besieged by enquirers wanting to be saved. Everywhere the presence and power of God's Spirit was felt. Then the work spread to the main city, Belfast, where whole suburbs crowded to prayer meetings and open-air meetings, and tens of thousands gathered to hear the gospel preached in the Botanical Gardens. It is estimated that a quarter of a million people were converted and added to the churches in Northern Ireland in the year 1859. Here is one description of this work of God: 'Drunkards, blasphemers, harlots, thieves on the one hand, and the respectable, the moral, the educated and the intelligent on the other, were instantaneously converted to a new way of life' (J. Edwin Orr, *The Second Evangelical Awakening in Britain*).

Soon, evangelists crossed the sea over to Scotland and England, and the revival spread through the whole of Britain so that more than a million people were added to its churches. Roy Coad describes what happened in the north-east of Scotland:

> James Turner, a fish-curer of Peterhead in North-East Scotland, was another man to be powerfully affected by the 1859 revival. Like M'Quilkin in Northern Ireland, he began to hold meetings for prayer, and a considerable movement of God broke out among the hardy fishermen of the district. Turner, praying one day, in his enthusiasm, for the conversion of all the

unconverted ministers and elders of Peterhead, was promptly excommunicated by the Kirk. The excommunication merely freed the energies of these enthusiastic men, and a powerful evangelistic movement sprang up along the coasts of Moray Firth. An ordinary fish-curing shed was used for the early meetings, and here Gordon Forlong the lawyer and "gentleman evangelist" from Aberdeen, and other leading evangelists, preached under lighted oil-lamps to an audience seated on rough planks of wood supported on fish barrels. The work in Peterhead was consolidated, and there grew up there some of the largest Brethren churches of Scotland'[40].

In the wake of the revival, many Brethren evangelists were raised up and sent out preaching the gospel. In the decades following the revival, they took the gospel to new parts of the country, planting assemblies throughout, and consolidating the work through teaching.

The 1859 revival was the third great historical event in the history of Brethren assemblies (after their founding in the late 1820s and their split into Open and Exclusive Brethren in 1848). This was because, as Robert Dann puts it, 'all denominations gained substantially, but it was the Brethren who gained the most, especially in Lancashire, Yorkshire and Northern Ireland'[41].

Thus, while in 1851 there were about 125 Open Brethren assemblies in England (according to the Religious Census taken that year[42]), yet by 1892, this number had increased to 723 open assemblies in England, a five-fold increase. In 1892, there were also 274 assemblies in Scotland, 156 in Ireland, and 32 in Wales, most of which did not exist before the 1859 revival.

The point of this history lesson is simple: God does powerful things when His people pray. We must also remember that revival is a sovereign work of God. God sends revival in His own time and according to His will – it cannot be drummed up on demand by us. Yet, on the other hand, revival is always preceded by prayer and propagated by gospel preaching.

The word 'revive' means 'to bring to life again'. Some Brethren do not like the word revival. This is very strange, seeing that we exist as the result of God reviving His work, not only in the 1820s but also in the 1859 revival. Revival is a biblical term, and a little acquaintance with the Bible shows why the word revival is so important. It is obvious that, spiritually, things go in cycles. There are periods when things prosper, like in David's reign, but there are also times of spiritual decline and failure. In the days of the Judges there are multiple cycles of spiritual departure and then revival as a Judge was raised up by God. The book of Nehemiah is about one of the great revivals in the Old Testament. Here we are going to look at its first chapter and learn some lessons about how God revives His work.

Nehemiah Chapter One – How Recovery Starts
Nehemiah is the story of a great work of God. In Nehemiah 4:2 the word 'revive' is used to describe this work of God. In this chapter, I suggest there are three important preconditions for God's work of revival.

Concern

In verses 1-2, Nehemiah is in Shushan in Persia when Hanani his brother and some others from Judea come, and Nehemiah asks them about the situation in Jerusalem. Why does Nehemiah ask? Because he cares. In reply, he is told five things about Jerusalem (vs 3-4):

1. the people of God are a remnant, few in number; they are described as 'the survivors who are left'.
2. they are 'there in great distress'.
3. they are also 'in reproach' – that is, mocked and despised by the Gentiles around them.
4. the wall of Jerusalem is also broken down, and
5. its gates are burned with fire.

The people of God were a dwindling remnant experiencing great difficulties, without any dignity or defence. Their future was not looking great. They almost resemble the state of God's work in many places today.

Here is where revival starts – with a realization of the great spiritual need we are in, whether individually or corporately. Do we care about the low state into which God's work has fallen? Are we troubled by the fact that many assemblies are weak and struggling to survive? Are we burdened for the millions of lost people around us who are going to perish in hell? Are we pained by the way in which God is entirely forgotten, or openly blasphemed, His truth is trodden underfoot, and His moral laws mocked and flouted?

Do you care? Is your heart pained at the spiritual conditions we see around us today? If you have read this far in the book, I hope that you do care about the honour of God's name, His truth, His work, and the spread of His gospel. Or are we more interested in other things: politics and sport, business and pleasure, travel and romance, making money and getting on in the world?

Humiliation
In verse 4 we have the next stage of revival. When Nehemiah heard this news, he sat down and wept, he mourned for days, fasting and praying before God.

Here we have a second great precondition for God to work. I am going to call it humiliation – humbling ourselves before God. Do you remember the famous words that God spoke to Solomon after the temple had been built? God appeared to him and said these words,

> When I shut up heaven and there is no rain, or command the locusts to devour the land, or send pestilence among My people, if My people who are called by My name will *humble* themselves, and pray and seek My face, and turn from their wicked ways, then I will hear from heaven, and will forgive their sin and heal their land (2 Chr. 7:13-14).

Why is humbling important? Because the great enemy of God's work is pride and complacency. Zephaniah warns that God will 'punish the men who are settled in complacency' (lit. on their lees) in Judah; he calls on them to gather to seek the Lord in humility (Zeph. 1:12-2:3). This is why some Christians dislike the word revival, because they like to pretend that everything is going well.

In their hearts they are comfortable and content. They hope that everything will be alright if they just sit tight and hold on. They say, 'the fault is not with us'. Their plea is this: 'stop all this talk of revival – it almost suggests that some things need to change'.

Spiritual pride is the great enemy of God's work because God hates pride. In Leviticus 26, where Israel was warned that if they did not obey Him, God would bring on them the curses of the Law, He says:

> And after all this, if you do not obey Me, then I will punish you seven times more for your sins. [19] I will break the ***pride*** of your power; I will make your heavens like iron and your earth like bronze. [20] And your strength shall be spent in vain; for your land shall not yield its produce, nor shall the trees of the land yield their fruit (Lev. 26:18-20).

Is this not an accurate description of what is happening in Brethren assemblies? We see very little fruit for our efforts in preaching the gospel – the heavens are like iron and the earth is like bronze. What is happening? God is breaking our pride.

Pride is the worst of all sins. It was Satan's sin, and the Pharisees' sin. And the worst sort of pride is spiritual pride. As C. S. Lewis said, besides pride, all other sins are mere flea-bites. Pride is dangerous because it blinds our eyes to our real problems – we do not see our faults, or listen to any criticism, even if the problems are obvious.

Here is Alexander Kurian:

Since this [great decline among the assemblies] is a wounding truth to our spiritual pride, we do not want to discuss it. It is painful, shameful and humbling to acknowledge and admit the decline and demise of the assemblies. But to my surprise, most assembly believers are not concerned about it. We still maintain a spiritual elitism, spiritual pride, and are critical of all other Christian groups[43].

Proud and complacent Christians are a hindrance to revival of God's work, either because they do not really care about the sad state of spiritual affairs, or they do not think that God is able to revive His work, or they think they are without fault before God so there is no need for any changes in their lives.

William MacDonald wrote this:

> Spiritually we are in a shocking condition. The status of many local fellowships is bad news, and deteriorating by the minute. "We have been arrogant, and have not rather mourned" – 1 Cor. 5:2. And that isn't all. We have become materialists to the core. We have become more proud of the number of successful businessmen in our churches than of the number of men of God. The dollar has become our master. ... We have become a status-seeking people. We sacrifice everything for prestige jobs, prestige homes and prestige cars. And we have prestige ambitions for our children...
>
> Too often we are living double lives. Outwardly

there is an appearance of piety and respectability. ... [but] in our personal lives there are coldness, bitterness, strife, gossip, back-biting and impurity. We are living a lie. Many of our children have [turned away from God to sin and the world – *or to other churches* – A.W.W.]. But are we broken before the Lord?

The sin of prayerlessness has been all too apparent. In our abounding wealth and self-sufficiency, we have not had any strong inward necessity driving us to prayer. Many of our prayer meetings need closing down...

And finally, there is our pride and impenitence. Rather than admit our low spiritual conditions, we endeavor to hide sin, to sweep it under the carpet where no one can see it. After all, we muse, time heals all things. ...

We are suffering a famine of the Word of God. The ministry lacks unction. Too often it is a rehash of the obvious. How seldom in meetings are we conscious that the Spirit of God has spoken to us in power? ... The worship meetings are often dead. Dull, awkward pauses are the fruit of prolonged occupation with the never-never land of TV. The evangelistic meetings are an exercise in futility: fishing in a bathtub where there are no fish. Years pass without the conversion of one single person...

We need to repent in our individual lives, to confess and forsake the sins that have brought us into this place of spiritual barrenness. We need to make right personal feuds and animosities, asking forgiveness from those we have wronged. And we need to repent as assemblies of God's people. Never in the memory of most of us has a meeting been called for the express purpose of repentance. And seldom in any of our meetings has confession ever been mentioned. But we need to do it. We desperately need to do it.[44]

We need to humble ourselves – to mourn, weep and fast. Why fasting? Fasting is about getting serious with God, a sign of repentance and mourning. By fasting, I refuse to enjoy myself, or live comfortably and normally, while this matter causes me so much spiritual pain. No more eating, drinking and being merry. The physical discomfort helps to focus our minds on our sin and need.

The evangelist Peter Brandon, who saw local revival two or three times, used to say that, in some situations, we should just stop our normal meetings. We should drop the pretence that everything is going well. We should get on our knees before God in repentance and prayer. But we prefer 'business as usual'.

In Isaiah 57:15, God said this: 'Thus says the High and Lofty One who inhabits eternity, whose name is Holy: "I dwell in the high and holy place, with him who has a contrite and humble spirit, to revive the spirit of the humble, and to revive the heart of the contrite ones"'. Here is where revival starts: with humiliation.

While some people are proud of their heritage and too arrogant to humble themselves, a second alternative to humbling ourselves before God is to try clever solutions to the decline we see in our churches. For example, in

1986, Nathan Smith wrote a book titled, *Roots, Renewal and the Brethren*, in which he analyzed the decline among American assemblies, and argued that the need for renewal was obvious. Even in 1986, this was undeniable.

Smith's suggested solution to the decline of the assemblies involved (a) hiring church consultants to suggest better ways of doing things using questionnaires and interviews, (b) developing strategies, (c) providing dynamic leadership, (d) developing small group fellowships, and finally (e) a whole chapter devoted to enhancing worship through more spontaneity, newer songs and updated musical styles[45].

I have grown up amongst a generation that thought the same way as Smith – that clever middle-management business strategies could solve the problem of assembly decline. But this is just another type of hubris – pride in our clever ideas. My generation cared deeply about the decline of assemblies, but thought that better organization, novel methods, or cool innovations could save the day. We loved to debate the minutiae: music, dress codes, Bible versions, and so on. Some of the criticisms were valid. But here is the snag: spiritual problems require spiritual solutions.

For example, ten times in the Bible we are told to 'sing a new song to the Lord'. While I love the older hymns of the faith, I also enjoy new songs that express the truths of the gospel and the glories of our Lord Jesus. But if we are interested in seeing true spiritual revival, changing song or music styles are not going to do much more than changing the carpet in the church building. My generation has tried to copy all sorts of clever tricks that other churches use to attract a crowd hoping to turn assemblies around. But this is not what God says to do. God says we need to turn to Him and humble ourselves.

The 'clever' suggestions for renewal my generation obsessed over were like an Israelite in the time of the Judges arguing that the solution to Israel's oppression was to engineer better chariots to use in battle against the Philistines. These 'solutions' entirely ignore the Divine Factor. God is the solution – not clever tricks. I am not saying that the problems my generation wrestled with are not real. But what I am saying is that trusting in our weapons is not the solution.

The only hope for revival in the days of the Judges, or in the days of the Kings, or in the days of Ezra and Nehemiah, or in the 1800s, or in our day today, is to turn to God with all our hearts in repentant, humble prayer and wait upon God to mightily revive His work. God has not changed the way He works. The solution is true spiritual revival – not gimmicks and the latest trendy fad. Here is how it happens: 'not by might, nor by power, but by My Spirit, says the Lord of hosts' (Zech. 4:6).

The early church was born out of a ten-day prayer meeting (Acts 1 and 2). The disciples were poor, uneducated men, without any human credentials – men who had denied and deserted their Lord. They realised that in their own strength or cleverness they were total failures and could never fulfil the Great Commission. So they cried out to God, for ten days straight, from the Ascension until Pentecost, to work mightily by His power. Every single true revival in the history of the church has come the same way: out of humble, repentant prayer which leads to preaching of the gospel – without clever human 'vision-casting', planning, networking, organizing, strategies, marketing, or fund-raising.

In 1949, there was a revival on the isle of Lewis, off the north-west coast of Scotland. Two house-bound old ladies in their eighties, one blind and the other arthritic, were burdened by the lack of young people in their church. So, twice a week, they would pray from 10 pm till 4 am in the morning. Then one of them had a vision of their church full of young people, so they got their minister and the elders to pray for two nights a week, in a barn.

This went on for over a month, until one of the men read Psalm 24 in the prayer meeting, 'Who shall ascend the hill of God? Who shall stand in His holy place? He that has clean hands and a pure heart'. He said, 'There is little point in praying like this if we do not have clean hands and a pure heart'. Then he prayed, 'God, are my hands clean? Is my heart pure?' and fell to the floor. God's people started humbling themselves before God, and after that prayer meeting, God started to work on the island.

There was an awareness of God and a conviction of sin. They asked a man to come and preach and the first night, 1000 people turned up under deep conviction of sin. He had to step over people kneeling on the floor crying out to God to get to the pulpit to preach. From there, revival spread across the island.

Prayer

Returning to Nehemiah 1:5-11, we have the third element of revival: prayer. Nehemiah's prayer is one of the great prayers of the Bible. This is where the work of God starts in earnest. Preacher Sidlow Baxter said this: 'I have pastored only three churches in my more than sixty years of ministry. We had revival in every one. And not one of them came as a result of my preaching. They came as a result of the membership entering into a covenant to pray until revival came. And it did come, every time'.

Notice seven things about Nehemiah's prayer. Firstly, there was intensity. Nehemiah starts and finishes his prayer in vs 5 and 11 with a strong word. Some Bibles translate it as 'I beseech', but in other places in the Old Testament it is almost a groan, 'O Lord', or 'alas'. Nehemiah is putting all his emotion into this prayer. It is 'fervent', 'earnest' prayer (James 5:16-17). In 1859, in the country district at the height of the blessing, they were having sixteen prayer meetings per day (100/week).

Second, observe the way Nehemiah addresses God in v5. He calls Him, 'Lord God of heaven, O great and awesome God'. Worship is an important part of revival. Once we catch a glimpse of God in His greatness, then real faith starts to pray. He is the God of heaven – ruling over all earthly affairs. He is the great God – there is nothing He cannot do. He is the awesome God, the One who is greatly to be feared. Contrast that with how Nehemiah refers to the Persian emperor in v11 – 'this man'. Nehemiah had a high view of God.

Third, Nehemiah's prayer involved confession. He

says the children of Israel have sinned, his father's house have sinned, and he had sinned. There is a personal examination and confession, and there is also corporate confession and intercession for his people Israel's sins.

Fourthly, in verses 8-9, notice the scriptural nature of Nehemiah's prayer. In true believing prayer, we recall God's promises and rest upon them, trusting in His faithfulness to fulfil them. Nehemiah quotes from the book of Deuteronomy where God promised that if Israel sinned, they would be scattered among the nations (i.e. the Babylonian exile), but if they returned to God, and kept His commands, God would regather them. Nehemiah is saying, God, You have promised in Your word to regather Israel to their land if they repent. So he placed his trust in God's promises in Scripture, looking to God to be faithful to His Word.

Fifthly, in verses 10-11, we see Nehemiah's faith. He says, God we are Your people who You redeemed by Your great power. Here Nehemiah is looking back in history to the Exodus, when God redeemed Israel from Egypt by His mighty hand. The implication is, You have rescued us before, Lord; do it again, by that same power.

Sixth, Nehemiah's prayer was corporate – see verse 11 – others had started to join him for prayer. Our Lord Jesus said, 'If two of you shall agree on earth concerning anything that they ask, it will be done for them by My Father in heaven' (Matt. 18:19). Why is corporate prayer important? Because in praying publicly, rather than doubting silently, we are taking a further step of faith.

Lastly, Nehemiah was persevering in prayer. In 1v1,

we read that he started praying in the month Kislev, and in 2v1 it is the month Nisan. He was fasting and praying for four months. He didn't give up. Instead, he persevered until God answered his prayers. We will look in more detail at the importance of prayer in a later chapter.

Conclusion

Revival is a spiritual work. God's work is not a humanly-devised or organized operation, like running a business. It is all about God's Spirit and His power. Paul describes it this way in 2 Corinthians 4:6-7:

> It is **God** who commanded light to shine out of darkness, who has shone in our hearts to give the light of the knowledge of the glory of God in the face of Jesus Christ. But we have this treasure in earthen vessels, that *the excellence of the power may be of God and not of us*.

Here is how revival starts: first there is a concern for God's work, then a humbling of ourselves in repentance and confession, which leads to prayer: fervent, worshipping, confessing, scriptural, believing, corporate, persevering prayer. When we seek God with all our hearts, God will respond and start to work. One of the great prayers in the Bible is in Psalm 90:16. Moses says, 'Let Your work appear to Your servants, and Your glory to their children'. This is what we need and what we want to see: God starting to work, for His glory.

Chapter Four

HOW GOD WORKS

In Habakkuk 3:2 the prophet prays, 'O LORD, revive Your work in the midst of the years, in the midst of the years make it known, in wrath remember mercy'. This is what we want to see: God reviving His work. But how does God work?

The assembly I have been part of for the last two years is located in a small country town (population 2500) in northern New South Wales, Australia. Most of the families in the assembly are involved in business, in farming or building and other trades. There are no super-spiritual people in our assembly, or great preachers. I have been involved in full-time Christian ministry for thirty years, and in most of the places I have been involved in serving the Lord, we have been happy if one person trusts in the Lord in a year. One convert means that our hard work has not been without fruit. Australia is like the hard ground in the parable of the Sower. Australian culture is very secular and anti-religious – people are materialistic pleasure seekers, with sport and recreation being the main gods. Church attendance in Australia is very low and most people have little interest in God.

Yet over the past ten years or so, the assembly has seen outsiders saved every year. In this past year, we have seen more than 20 people evangelized, virtually all from non-church backgrounds. Over a dozen of them have professed faith in Christ. We have had more than a dozen baptisms. Many of these people are middle-aged men – normally the most unlikely people in Australia to come to Christ. When one visiting speaker heard about the number of people turning to the Lord, he said, 'You almost have a revival happening there, ***and we need it***'.

Why is all this blessing happening? First, let me say it is not because of me. Let me make it quite clear that I am mainly a Bible teacher. Nor is the blessing because of some other great visiting evangelist or preacher. We have not conducted a gospel campaign. Nor is it because of some special evangelistic opportunity – like a nearby university which provides an avenue for outreach. People have come to faith through multiple different members of the assembly reaching them with the gospel. These converts come from all different walks of life and have all been contacted in different ways.

John 3:8 says that 'the Spirit blows where it wishes'. That is, God works wherever and in whatever way He pleases. There might be some special reason the Lord has been blessing our assembly's outreach that we don't know about. But, from a biblical perspective, I think there are four factors involved. Let me explain.

If every assembly in Australia was seeing ten people saved every year, there would be no need to write about revival. We would see 20,000 people added to our churches in a decade. But I believe that the four principles we will look at in this chapter are transferable to any other assembly or situation, regardless of culture, because they are the basic biblical principles of revival.

In this chapter, we will look at Nehemiah chapter 2. The principles of revival in Nehemiah are exactly the same principles that are behind the blessing we are seeing in God's work in our small country town.

Prayer

The first principle – which we have already seen from Nehemiah 1 – is prayer. The assembly I belong to has a lot of prayer, probably more than any assembly I have ever been in before. Here is the secret of blessing: prayer. Because of Covid lockdown restrictions, we had lots of people meeting for prayer in pairs. Then in the lead-up to our Christmas Carol outreach last year, we had a week of early morning prayer meetings, in addition to our normal prayer meetings. Then, in the week after Christmas, several brothers prayed together every afternoon. What was the result? In the months between Christmas and Easter, we had fourteen people who agreed to do an evangelistic course which took them through the gospel message over six weeks. A number of these have professed to trust Christ as their Saviour. If we were to deny that there was a link between our prayer meetings at Christmas and the blessing we have seen in the early part of this year, we might as well give up being Christians altogether and declare ourselves atheists. God is answering prayer. Do you want to see blessing in your church? Start by getting serious about prayer. Having one assembly prayer meeting a week is not enough. It needs to be more like once a day!

What Happens when God's People Pray

Revival requires more than prayer. Spurgeon said that action without prayer is presumption, but prayer without action is hypocrisy. In the previous chapter, we saw that Nehemiah was a man of prayer. Nehemiah chapter 2 shows us what God did in answer to Nehemiah's prayers.

God Opens Doors

In chapter 2 verses 1-4, God opens a door, an opportunity, for Nehemiah to go and rebuild the walls of Jerusalem. Nehemiah appeared before the king looking sad. When the king asked what the matter was, Nehemiah became dreadfully afraid, presumably because he might be accused of plotting to harm or poison the king. But after assuring the king of his loyalty by wishing him long life, Nehemiah took the opportunity to speak about rebuilding Jerusalem: "Why shouldn't I be sad – the city of my fathers' tombs lies in ruins!"

At this, in verse 4, the king said, So what do you ask? God had answered his prayer. He had opened a door for Nehemiah to make his request.

This is the way that God works in the New Testament too: God opens doors when His people pray. In Acts 2, the disciples had been praying for 10 days, and God poured out His Spirit on the Day of Pentecost, so that through the miracle of the gift of tongues, Peter preached and 3000 souls were saved. In Acts 3, God opened a door for Peter and John to preach – as they went to pray – and more people were saved. In Acts 16, Paul and Silas crossed into Europe, but the doors seemed closed at

Philippi. They went down to the river to pray, and God opened the heart of Lydia to listen to the gospel. Then God opened the doors of the prison by an earthquake while they prayed, and the jailer was saved. This is how God works – as his people pray, God opens doors.

God gives boldness
God also gave Nehemiah boldness. After the king asked what Nehemiah wanted, he sent up a quick 'arrow' prayer to God. Then Nehemiah asked the king to allow him to go back to Jerusalem to rebuild it. In vs 7-8, after the King had granted his request, Nehemiah boldly asked for letters of permission to pass through territory and letters of permission to acquire timber for rebuilding.

In a similar way to Nehemiah, we are not going to see people reached and saved with the gospel unless we have the boldness to speak to people about the Lord. We can't forever 'beat about the bush'.

But often we feel so lacking in courage we don't speak up for God, even when opportunities arise. However the wonderful thing is that God doesn't ask us to do things in our own strength. If we pray, God will gives us boldness. This was true in the early church too (see Acts 4:23-33).

In our assembly, we have seen more than twenty non-Christian people evangelised over the last year, that is, contacted and clearly presented with the gospel message. More than a dozen of them have professed faith in Christ. How did this happen? Through Christians boldly speaking to friends in the community about spiritual things, and then inviting them to learn about who Jesus is, what He did, and how He relates to people today.

How do Christians become bold enough to speak to non-Christians and invite them to explore the gospel message? Through prayer, God opens opportunities to speak. As they see God at work in the witness of other Christians, they take courage and speak up for Christ too.

God gives Wisdom
God also gave Nehemiah wisdom. In verse 12, Nehemiah writes of 'what my God had put in my heart to at Jerusalem'. We have already seen his wisdom in his requests for letters of permission to pass through to Judea and for the supply of timber. Nehemiah had done his homework – he had heard about the opponents of the Jews in the region beyond the river and he had also thought about what rebuilding Jerusalem would involve, and he asked the king for timber to be supplied, even naming the official who was responsible.

Further, in vs11-16, when Nehemiah arrived in Jerusalem, after three days he went out by night and surveyed the damage to the walls. Notice Nehemiah's secrecy: going out at night, taking only a few servants, and only one animal – too many animals, and people might have heard their noise. Nehemiah wanted to see how bad the damage was in the most difficult parts of the rebuilding program – where the valley was steepest. Verse 16 tells us that Nehemiah did not tell anyone about his plan until he had gathered his information.

Imagine if Nehemiah had come to Jerusalem, and announced that he was going to rebuild the walls, but some skeptical official had stood up and said, Sorry, Nehemiah, this idea sounds nice but you obviously don't know the first thing about the walls of Jerusalem, and the difficulties involved. Nehemiah and his plan could have been discredited before he started. Wisdom requires gathering knowledge. There is a lot of wisdom in Nehemiah's actions here.

The same is true of God's work today. We need to use wisdom as well as being bold in sharing the gospel. Holding a Sunday evening gospel meeting (as many assemblies have done in years gone by) where the only hearers are seats and saints is not actually preaching the gospel – because no unsaved people are hearing it.

We are never going to see anybody saved if we have no contact with non-Christians. We must get alongside people and get to know them to share the gospel with them. If we do not share the gospel personally, we cannot invite them to hear the gospel in public meetings. People in Australia are very wary of attending a church, and it takes personal contact and friendship to open up opportunities to speak for the Lord.

How were people contacted here? Our assembly uses many ways to make contact with people in the community, and the twenty or more people we have evangelised over the last year have been initially contacted in different ways: some through our Christmas Carol service, some through a café we run one morning a week, some through tracts put in letterboxes, one through a Bible left in a local coffee shop, some through our Youth Group, one family through our midweek children's outreach, some through local flood recovery relief, some through a funeral service held in our church building, and some just through people speaking to friends.

How were people presented with the gospel? In our church, we still hold a monthly Sunday evening gospel meeting where we preach the gospel, but we call it a family barbecue, and often have it at peoples' homes; we provide a meal and invite non-Christian friends to attend, where we give a short 15-20 minute gospel message. We believe in public preaching, but we also realise that many people in Australia today are so thoroughly ignorant of the Bible that the truths of the gospel are not easily or quickly understood. So, we invite people to do a course called Christianity Explained. Why? Because:

1. it is done in a home alongside the person rather than in a church building,
2. it is done over six weeks because the gospel contains many concepts that need to be carefully explained to non-Christians, including who Christ is, why He died, the fact of His resurrection, that salvation is not by works but by grace, and through faith.
3. because it allows people to ask questions,
4. because it asks them to read the Gospel of Mark and encounter Christ for themselves, and
5. because over these six weeks they build up a friendship with the Christian

The apostles not only preached the gospel publicly but also privately, from 'house to house' (Acts 20:20), and in our situation, the personal approach seems to yield more results. Wisdom involves doing what works. Someone has said that the definition of insanity is doing the same thing over and over and expecting different results.

I am not saying that what works for us here is how other people must evangelize, or that other approaches to preaching the gospel will not work. It is not a matter of putting our trust in some method of evangelism – we must put our trust in God and His gospel. Preaching the gospel boldly and yet with wisdom requires that we do not simply try to do what worked one hundred years ago, or what other people are doing in other places or cultures. The apostles used different approaches in different cities where they preached the gospel. When there was no synagogue to publicly preach in, they spoke to individuals wherever they could. We too need to use wisdom in preaching the gospel so that we see people being saved.

Practical Kindness to the Poor and Needy

A third factor involved in seeing people saved was helping people whose homes were damaged in a local flood. Jesus our Lord was characterized by good works (Acts 10:38) and commands us to be too (Matthew 5:16, Titus 2:14). Good works not only show the love of God, but open doors for the gospel. *Start doing them*!

The Power of God's Spirit.

I hope you are starting to see a pattern in this chapter: if we are people of prayer, who care for others, God will open up opportunities, God will give us boldness to speak, and God will give us the wisdom we need too. God doesn't ask us to do His work in our wisdom, or in our own strength. Instead, if we pray, God will start to work.

Prayer is the most important part of our work for God.

Someone called Jeremy Taylor once said, 'Since the days of Pentecost, has the whole church ever put aside every other work and waited upon Him for ten days, that the Spirit's power might be manifested? We give too much attention to method and machinery and resources and too little to the source of the power'.

Here is the crucial lesson we learn from this chapter: God does not ask us to work for Him. Instead God wants to work through us. It is not us doing something for God – it is God doing His work as we pray and actively obey. This is what we want, and need: God at work.

Our Lord Jesus Christ said, 'I will build my church' (Matt. 16:18). Not 'you will build My church'. It is Christ working, through us. In our weakness His strength is made perfect. As we depend on God in earnest prayer, God opens the way before us, and fit us and fills us to do that work. This is how God works.

We must be committed to spiritual power for our success. To understand what I mean, listen to what Professor Arthur Rendle-Short says about the 'divine factor'. He is here writing about missionary work, but the principle applies equally to evangelism in church life:

> The success of foreign mission work does not depend on business methods, nor even on the number and intelligence of the workers maintained in a given district; it is exactly related to spiritual power. Spiritual power is only obtained by following spiritual methods. A real outpouring of the Spirit accomplishes far more in a few weeks than diligent teaching and preaching can do in as many years; it comes here and there

mysteriously, but only where there are spiritual men and women working on spiritual lines. We stake everything on the divine factor[46].

Chapter 2 might at first sight appear to be Nehemiah doing things. But actually, it is God at work all the way through. Twice (in vs 8 and 18), Nehemiah spoke of 'the (good) hand of my God upon me'. The king's favours and Nehemiah's success were a sign of God's gracious answer to prayer. It was the 'Divine Factor'.

In conservative Brethren assemblies, we believe in (and often experience) being led by God's Spirit in worshipping Christ. But we do not seem to believe in being led by the Spirit in gospel work. We believe in our trusty 'program' – the Sunday evening gospel meeting (that no outsiders have been saved at for many years), or Sunday School (which few attend). Progressive assemblies have tried clever new outreach 'programs' for years, using technology (radio, TV, internet), literature, music, camps, sport, hobbies, food. None of these are wrong, but we wear ourselves out with hard work for little fruit. (Note: God will bless all gospel effort, however we do it). But the solution is not in our programs, ancient or modern, clever or not. We need to pray, and let the Holy Spirit lead.

What we do is this: we set up a 'program' and pray for God to bless it. But God tells us to humble ourselves before Him in repentant, earnest, believing prayer, and the Spirit of God will guide and direct us, opening up opportunities for evangelism, so we see souls saved.

Personal Walk with God

There is one final factor in God's work: personal godliness. Remember what Rendle-Short wrote:

> Spiritual power is only obtained ... where there are spiritual men and women working on spiritual lines.

We see Nehemiah's godliness throughout chapter 2. He continually trusts God, asks for God's help, gives God all the glory, and even answers the mockery of the Jews' enemies in v20 with the confident words, 'The God of heaven Himself will prosper us'.

Nehemiah was a man who walked with God. Three times in this chapter he speaks of 'my God'. The same is true wherever we look in the Bible: God works through people who are walking with Him.

Walking with God has two sides to it. Firstly, we must be people who are spending quality time with God every day. Just reading 'Our Daily Bread' (rather, Our Daily Crumb), and having 'a little talk with Jesus' is not enough.

Listen to the secret of George Müller's spiritual health and vitality, and bear in mind that this was a discovery he made after a number of years in full-time ministry:

> I saw more clearly than ever, that the first great and primary business to which I ought to attend every day was to have my soul happy in the Lord. The first thing to be concerned about was not how much I might serve the Lord, or how I might glorify the Lord; but how I might get my soul into a happy state, and how my inner man might be nourished.

So what did George Müller do? Prior to this, his practice was to get up and pray first thing in the morning, but his mind often wandered, so that he wasted time and wasn't praying at all. Müller decided on a change. He decided to get up very early every morning and read God's Word, and after a few minutes he was led into thanking God, or confessing sin, or interceding for others. Now he realised that the most important thing in his day was to give himself to reading and meditating on God's Word so his heart might be comforted, encouraged, taught, warned, or corrected, so that his heart might be brought into communion with God. But the result was that his prayer life also became more effective too. (By the way, he started going to bed early!).

This was also the most important lesson I learned in Christian ministry from the two evangelists I helped in my twenties in Tottenham, London. They used to get up at 5.30 am every morning to meditate in God's Word and pray. It is not always easy to put this into practice, particularly if you have small children, or your health is not great. But this is the way to blessing in our individual lives: getting up early every day to sit at Jesus' feet.

If we are going to be useful for God, we need to be filled with His Spirit. What does this involve? It means that we are going to have to 'let the Word of Christ dwell in us richly' (Col. 3:16 – notice how this verse parallels being 'filled with the Spirit' in Ephesians 5:18). We are going to have to be people of prayer, asking (like Paul) that God 'would grant you, according to the riches of His glory, to be strengthened with power through His Spirit in the inner man, that Christ may dwell in your hearts through faith ... that you may be filled with all the fullness of God. (Eph. 3:16-19). We are going to have to be busy serving God. All this is involved in being spiritual people, filled with God's Spirit.

The second aspect of walking with God is that we need to be sanctified, that is, separated to God. Let's put it this way: If we want to be filled with the Spirit, then we must not let other things fill our lives. Someone has said, 'If you are not filled with the Spirit, what are you filled with'? If we fill our minds with the things of the world – its business, politics, sport, entertainment, and so on – we will not be in communion with God. If we wish to see our prayers answered, we must be 'lifting up *holy* hands, without wrath and doubting' (1 Tim. 2:8). We must forgive others, and be living in fellowship with God's people, turning away from sin and asking God's forgiveness for it.

Conclusion

Nehemiah is a story of God at work. This is what we want above all – the presence and power of God Himself at work among us. We don't want to be straining and struggling in our own strength, or wisdom. We want to see God at work. If so, we need to follow Nehemiah's example and be people who walk with God, people of prayer, and people who depend on the power of His Spirit for opportunities to serve Him, for boldness and wisdom.

Chapter Five

HOW TO PRODUCE HEALTHY CHRISTIANS

In the 18th century, George Whitefield and John Wesley were raised up by God to preach the gospel in the British Isles and in America in what is often called the Great Awakening, a great outpouring of the Holy Spirit in revival. J. R. Green, in his book, *A Short History of the English People*, wrote:

> A religious revival burst forth ... which changed in a few years the whole temper of English society. The Church was restored to life and activity. Religion carried to the hearts of the people a fresh spirit of moral zeal, while it purified our literature and our manners. A new philanthropy reformed our prisons, infused clemency and wisdom into our penal laws, abolished the slave-trade, and gave the first impulse to popular education[47].

Of the two men, Whitefield is considered the greater preacher. However, as far as long-term results are concerned, there was a great difference between Wesley and Whitefield. Wesley's followers eventually formed the Methodist Church and his work lived on for many years, whereas Whitefield lamented that his followers were 'a rope of sand'. By that he meant they were mere individual believers disconnected and unable to support each other. The difference between the two men was that Whitefield concentrated mostly on preaching the gospel, while Wesley not only preached the gospel, but also gathered his converts in weekly 'classes' where they would encourage and strengthen each other in their faith. The result is that, today, while many Christians have heard of John Wesley, the name George Whitefield means nothing to most Christians.

So far in this book, we have looked at the decline of Brethren assemblies, and considered what the Bible teaches about how to revive God's work: through prayer and active gospel outreach. Now, we turn to consider the question of why Brethren assemblies in the Western world are in decline.

Some believers' reaction to such a question is to point to external or societal factors (like immigration, the sexual revolution, the invention of TV, affluence, or the charismatic movement). But, as we have seen, other evangelical churches have not suffered the same decline as Brethren assemblies and, in fact, other evangelical churches continue to grow despite these factors. It is only Roman Catholicism, liberal churches and the Brethren that are in dramatic decline in the West.

Nor is it possible to point to a few 'bad apple' assemblies that are struggling and closing because of local problems. It is rather the opposite: only the occasional assembly is doing well – most are struggling. The decline is general, not local. The problem is structural and systemic. Are there any obvious reasons for the decline? I believe there are.

To understand what is happening, we are going to turn to 1 Timothy, a letter that might be described as a trouble-shooting manual for churches.

Spiritual Health

As we turn to 1 Timothy, I want to focus on an expression found in 1 Timothy 1:10: 'sound doctrine'. We sometimes use the word 'sound' to mean correct or true – as in, teaching that does not contain errors. But that is not what the word 'sound' really means. The best way to understand this word is to see it in Greek: *hygieno*. We get our English word hygiene from it. The Greek word *hygieno* means to be healthy. *Hygieno* is used nine times in the pastoral epistles (1 and 2 Timothy and Titus). In 1 Timothy 6:3, we read of 'wholesome (Gk. *hygieno*) words', i.e. good for your health. This is what 'sound' means – wholesome, health-promoting. By contrast, in 1 Timothy 6:4, Paul warns of some who are 'obsesssed (Gk. *nosos*, literally 'sick', cf. Matt. 4:23) with disputes and arguments'.

Spiritual health is extremely important to Paul in the pastoral epistles, because spiritual health is very important in the church. If you have a church full of unhealthy Christians, you have a church that is in trouble. Unhealthy Christians don't worship, or evangelise, or pray, or love others – instead they will grumble, squabble, fight, and fall out with each other, or leave and go elsewhere over a personal slight, a minor difference of opinion, or some other ruffling of their feathers.

On the other hand, if a church is producing healthy Christians, the result will be that the believers will worship, pray, evangelise, and love others. If we get this right – if we are producing healthy Christians – everything else in the life of the church will do well. Spiritual health is central and foundational to a flourishing church life.

In 1 Timothy 4, Paul devotes a whole chapter to how believers can be spiritually healthy. Firstly, by having good diet. In 1 Timothy 4:6 he says, 'If you instruct the brethren in these things, you will be a good minister of Jesus Christ, nourished in the words of faith and of the good doctrine which you have carefully followed'. The word 'nourished here means 'fed'.

Secondly, in 4:7 Paul talks about the need for exercise. He says, 'exercise yourself rather to godliness, for bodily exercise profits a little, but godliness is profitable for all things, having promise of the life that is now and of that which is to come'.

In verses 12-16, Paul speaks about the third element of spiritual health: growth. He addresses Timothy in verse 12 as a 'youth' ('Let no one despise your youth') and in verse 15 he says, 'let your progress – your advance, your development - be evident to all'. On the other hand, he warns against spiritual neglect in verse 14: 'Do not neglect the gift in you'. We are to be growing in spiritual maturity, and in using our spiritual gifts.

Here is why Brethren assemblies are declining: because we have a problem with spiritual health. We are either not well fed, or not exercising ourselves, or not growing and developing in maturity and gift.

Instead of producing spiritually healthy Christians, we have people who leave, one after another, generation after generation, in assemblies across the Western world, until eventually there are only a few old folk left, and then these assemblies close down. We need to understand why we have this spiritual health crisis.

Here is what a medical autopsy report reveals about a dead patient: this person was not healthy. The same is true of the majority of Brethren assemblies that have closed: they had a spiritual health problem. But why are Brethren assemblies not producing healthy Christians?

The Importance of Teaching in the Church

So far, we have seen that Paul is concerned about the matter of spiritual health. What was Paul's remedy for spiritual ill-health in the church? We see it in 1 Timothy 1:1-10: 'sound teaching', that is, health-promoting teaching. The expression 'sound teaching' (or 'sound words' or 'wholesome words') is found six times in the Pastoral Epistles. Here is one secret to healthy Christians: they get enough healthy food. Look at 1 Timothy 1:3-5:

> As I urged you when I went into Macedonia-- remain in Ephesus that you may charge some that they teach no other doctrine, nor give heed to fables and endless genealogies, which cause disputes rather than godly edification[48] which is in faith. Now the purpose of the commandment is love from a pure heart, from a good conscience, and from sincere faith.

Good teaching is an important key to producing healthy Christians. This is why Paul left Timothy in Ephesus – to deal with teaching in the church. Paul did not leave Timothy in Ephesus to evangelise, or to deal with division or a case of discipline. This shows us how vitally important teaching was to Paul. In verses 3-5, Paul outlines five benefits of good, healthy teaching:

1. It results in godly edification (v4b). That is, good healthy teaching builds God's people up in their faith so that there is godly order, whereas false-teaching and poor-quality teaching produces disputes and arguments (see verse 4).
2. In v5, we read that the purpose of Paul's command (for Timothy to stay and teach in Ephesus) is love. Christians who are well taught and well fed demonstrate the fruit of a healthy Christian life: love.
3. The result of good teaching is a pure heart (that is, a clean heart, v5). Good teaching results in hearts that are cleansed from sin. How does this happen? Good teaching has a corrective effect upon our lives, so that we deal with sin, and live cleaner, purer lives.
4. Healthy teaching results in a good conscience, v5. This is not the same as a clean conscience. A good conscience is a conscience in good working order. Good teaching results in Christians who are more discerning between right and wrong, who are more sensitive to sin in their own lives, who fear God and do good.

5. Lastly, the result is sincere, unhypocritical faith, v5. That is, the believers are living, not as hypocrites, but with a strong, lively faith.

Wouldn't this be great – if all of God's people, instead of disputing and squabbling (see v4), were full of love, with clean hearts, discerning minds, and demonstrating vibrant faith.

We further notice, in verses 6-7, that not all teaching in the church is health-promoting teaching. It is possible to have teaching in the church, but still not really see any life changing results in God's people. Paul writes that:

> from which some, having strayed, have turned aside to idle talk, desiring to be teachers of the law, understanding neither what they say nor the things which they affirm (1 Tim. 1:6-7)

Some preaching is academic, dry and lifeless, without relevance or application. Some other teaching, v6, is 'vain jangling' (KJV), 'idle talk' (NKJ), 'vain babbling' (Darby's translation). It is just empty jabber-jaw. My grandfather used to describe this as preachers with buckets of words, but thimbles of thoughts. It is preaching that does not hold the attention of listeners, but rather rambles aimlessly all over the place, lacking any structure and making it up as it goes.

In verse 7 we see another sort of poor-quality preaching. There we some Jewish legalists in Ephesus who liked to think of themselves as teachers, but who didn't understand the Bible very well. So they strongly affirmed things that were not true, desiring to be teachers of the law. There are still Christians like that today – rather than building up God's people on the solid truths of Scripture, they flog their pet hobby-horses and humanly-devised rules.

C. H. Spurgeon said that the day will come when instead of shepherds feeding sheep, we will have clowns entertaining goats. Some preaching is merely entertaining – a cross between stand-up comedy and a self-help seminar. It is ear-tickling – lots of jokes and anecdotes, but little mention of the gospel realities of sin, death, judgment, eternity, the need for repentance or the glories of Christ. Some other preaching is false-teaching, it is flat-out wrong – it might be going beyond Scripture, or not properly balancing Scripture against Scripture. All these sorts of teaching are dangerous.

So 'sound doctrine', that is healthy teaching, is an important part of this process of growing healthy Christians. There are some churches that think that if they have got their diary filled with preachers' names that they are doing their job. But a lot of teaching doesn't actually produce growing, healthy Christians. So, how do we get healthy teaching?

How they did their Teaching in the New Testament

We are nearly ready to discuss why there is a spiritual health problem in so many Brethren assemblies, and we have suggested that the reason has something to do with teaching. But before we look at the problem, we need to notice one other thing that 1 Timothy 1:3-7 shows us.

Notice four things about how New Testament churches like Ephesus did their teaching:

1. From verse 3 we learn that there were multiple teachers in the church. Paul says that Timothy is to tell *some* not to teach false-doctrine. That word 'some' is in the plural. There were multiple teachers teaching false-doctrine. But they were only some of the teachers – not all. There were others giving sound, healthy teaching. The NT church did not just have one man doing all the preaching and teaching. There were multiple teachers.
2. There was freedom and opportunity for people to use their gifts in church. Nowhere is Timothy given the job of choosing speakers (nor does Paul tell the elders to do this), and we can see from this passage that some people were exceedingly poor preachers, given to idle babbling (v7) and even worse. They were free to speak on subjects of their own choosing. Some of them were teaching false doctrine while others were given to useless speculation and silly fables (v4).
3. However, the preaching was subject to public evaluation and critique, with preachers being held to account for the quality of their messages. Timothy was to model good preaching, but also to silence false-teaching and challenge poor preaching.
4. Timothy was not told to do all the teaching. Timothy was not the first bishop of Ephesus (as the KJV footnote says), nor was he Senior Pastor Tim, the Teaching Pastor at Ephesus. There was no such thing in the New Testament. Nor was Timothy told to

choose the speakers, or choose the subjects for some consecutive teaching plan. This might be our immediate response to such a situation: get rid of those teaching false-doctrine or long-winded bores, and substitute some consecutive teaching program. But Timothy is not told to do this.

Here we come to the first major problem that, I suggest, has led to spiritually unhealthy Brethren assemblies and their closure: the 'open meeting'. Now, please understand that I am not saying that the 'open meeting' itself is the problem, or that it is unbiblical, or that the early Brethren misinterpreted the Bible when they started having meetings like this. The very opposite is true.

The Open Meeting is Biblical

It is not just in 1 Timothy that we read about church meetings that were like this. 1 Corinthians 14:26-40 also teaches that church meetings are participatory and interactive. William MacDonald in his *Believer's Bible Commentary* writes:

> What happened when the early church came together? It appears from [1 Cor. 14] verse 26 that the meetings were very informal and free. There was liberty for the Spirit of God to use the various gifts which He had given to the Church. One man, for instance, would read a psalm and then another would set forth some teaching ... Paul gives tacit approval to this "open meeting" where there was liberty for the Spirit of God to speak through different brothers. But

having stated this, he sets forth the first control in the exercise of these gifts. Everything must be done with a view to edification'[49].

It is not just Brethren commentators who see it like this. Virtually every commentator on 1 Corinthians agrees with MacDonald. Thus, the Anglican Leon Morris, commentating on 1 Corinthians 14:26-40, writes:

> this little paragraph is very important as giving us the most intimate glimpse we have of the early church at worship ... it is our earliest account of a service and it enables us to see something of what the first Christians actually did when they assembled to worship God. Clearly their services were more spontaneous and less structured than was normally the case in later days[50].

Gordon Fee writes, 'What is striking in this entire discussion is the absence of any mention of leadership or of anyone who would be responsible for seeing that these guidelines were generally adhered to. The community appears to be left to itself and to the Holy Spirit'[51].

Methodist theologian Howard Marshall, writing about a similar passage in 1 Thessalonians 5:19-21 ('Do not quench the Spirit, do not despise prophecies, test all things, hold fast what is good') argues: 'What is set out in detail in 1 Cor. 12-14 is stated here summarily. The Spirit is powerful and active like fire in the congregation (cf. Rom. 12:11, 2 Tim. 1:6 for the metaphor). Gifts for ministry were being exercised, but some people were trying to suppress them (we don't know just how), but it is wrong to do so'[52].

F. F. Bruce writes that 1 Corinthians 14:33b ('as in all the churches of the saints'), 'means that the order prescribed for the church at Corinth is that followed by other churches, especially in Paul's mission field'[53].

Notice Bruce's word 'prescribed'. Some people argue that the 'open meeting' in 1 Timothy and 1 Corinthians 14 is merely descriptive, not prescriptive. That is, the Bible is merely telling us what happened, not saying that we should do things the same way. Others argue that Paul was not commending the idea of the 'open meeting', but instead criticizing it. But this is not true, for Paul does not tell Timothy to get rid of the 'open meeting', despite its challenges. Instead, in 1 Corinthians 14:37, Paul writes that the guidelines for church gatherings he has given are 'the commandments of the Lord'. 1 Corinthians 14:26-40 is one of the most prescriptive passages in the New Testament, with no less than fourteen imperatives (i.e. commands) giving guidelines for the 'open meeting'. Others argue that 1 Corinthians 14 merely says that we need order in church (v40). But it also teaches that believers have the freedom – the right – to use their spiritual gifts in church.

This is why the early Brethren practised an 'open meeting'. Even though their gatherings were radically different from what other churches did, they wanted to follow what God says about church in Scripture (not human traditions or humanly-organised programs).

Professor Rendle-Short wrote:

When Paul heard what painful meetings they were having at Corinth, he might have said, "Do not listen any longer to all these ignorant people, mostly slaves. Make Stephanas your minister, and let him do it all." No doubt this would have helped very much in some directions, but the Apostle was not prepared to give up the open meeting. It was far too valuable. He did not want to make churches like comets, with a brilliant head and a long nebulous tail. He told them, however, and it is very important to put the injunction into practice, that the assembly was not called upon to listen to everybody who chose to make himself a nuisance, or who talked unprofitably. There were some " whose mouths must be stopped " (Titus I. 11). The listeners were to be the judges (I Cor. 14. 27-29). Nor were two to take part at the same time. There was liberty but not licence. It was an open meeting, but there were rules to be observed. It was a meeting open for the Spirit to speak by whom He would, not open for men to say what they pleased[54].

Early Brethren Problems with the Open Meeting

Even in the early days of the Brethren they had to wrestle with problems in the 'open meeting'. Lord Congleton (John Parnell, one of the founders of the Brethren in Dublin in the 1820s) wrote a booklet called *The Open Meeting* (published in 1877). In it he mentioned how Müller had tried the open meeting in Teignmouth and then abandoned it, because of its problems. Later on, however, Müller returned to an open meeting at Bristol.

Sir Robert Anderson left the Brethren, in his words, because of 'their unwillingness to provide intelligent ministry at meetings other than the Lord's Table, and their haphazard way of doing things'[55]. The same was apparently true of Thomas Barnardo, founder of the famous Barnado's orphan work[56]. Grattan Guinness, the Irish evangelist, who was associated with the Brethren at Merrion Hall, Dublin, but later left them, wrote a booklet against the 'open meeting'[57].

The open meeting was an early cause of dispute between Darby and Newton at Plymouth, which led eventually to the division between Open and Exclusive Brethren. Newton had 'a growing conviction that Brethren 'open' meetings were uniquely prone to disorder ... [so] to maintain order at the meetings and restrain ungifted contributors ... he was appointed as presiding elder'[58]. The meeting at Plymouth (by 1843, about 1000 strong) was still 'open' for different brethren to participate, as Newton described it:

> Every Lord's Day morning we meet for communion at the Lord's Table. It is a meeting open to the ministry of any whom God may have gifted for such service: there are generally three or four brethren present, who are known either to speak or to pray to edification in the congregation ... We believe it to be their duty to stir up the gift that is in them. But whilst we thus expect the regular ministry of some, pauses are allowed to occur, which afford the opportunity of rising gifts, if such there be, to be developed and proved. If any

speak, and after the trial their speaking is not found to edification, the Brethren who are regarded as addicted to the ministry of the Saints here ... wait on the individual and advise him, or if the case needs, request him not to minister. We have not had occasion to act thus more than four or five times during fourteen years, but when we have been obliged to adopt this course, we have never found it to fail'[59].

Later, however, Newton and another brother, Harris, preached week about, with little time left for the Lord's supper, and the entire meeting organised[60]. This led to friction with Darby, who accused Newton of clericalism.

Later in Müller's life, the open meeting had its problems at Bristol. Some complained that the ministry was too often devoted to prophetic or practical topics, rather than dealing with the full range of scriptural subjects. Another complaint was that various businessmen and ex-military men who were not very gifted were indulged by Müller because they generously supported his orphan work financially. In other words, there was not enough oversight of the open meeting by the elders, so that it might be more profitable.

Anthony Norris Groves himself, who had first stated the principle of the open meeting in Dublin in the 1820s, later argued that it needed to be properly regulated and balanced. He said, 'I greatly approve and value a fixed ministry, but will ever protest against an exclusive one'. By this Groves meant a 'careful blend of formal teaching prepared by gifted men and informal contributions from any whom the Spirit might lead' (Dann, p404). Groves stated, 'for myself, I would join no church permanently that had not some constituted rule. I have seen enough of that plan, of everyone doing what is right in his own eyes and then calling it the Spirit's order, to feel assured it is a delusion'. Robert Dann writes, 'Groves, Müller and others took the trouble to prepare beforehand – a Scripture to read and explain, some thoughts on a devotional theme, a testimony, an exhortation, a hymn appropriate to their particular circumstances. But along with this went freedom for a spontaneous response from any who found themselves uplifted by what they heard. Groves made it his aim "to try and impress upon every member of Christ's body that he has some ministry given him for the body's edification – and instead of depressing, encouraging each one to come forward and serve the Lord". In New Testament times, he noted, "there was positively no limitation whatever on the right of every individual brother teaching, preaching and administering the sacraments, without asking leave either of the apostles or anyone else ... Every man's duty is to minister according to the ability that God giveth". This emphasis on "liberty of ministry" was one of Norris Groves's greatest legacies to the church of Christ'[61].

The early Brethren not only had an open meeting (normally held on Sunday mornings), but also evening meetings. These evening meetings were not usually 'open meetings', but had an appointed preacher. Normally these were gospel meetings, but not always. For example, the very large assembly at Hereford divided in 1850 over whether the Sunday evening meeting should be for gospel preaching or Bible teaching. Percy Hall took the view that it should be for Bible teaching, and left the assembly with many others. By the way, the morning meeting at Hereford lasted from 10:30 till 1 pm (two and a half hours). This is because it included ample opportunity for 'open' Bible teaching.

Many of the early Brethren assemblies also had resident preachers – what Groves meant by a 'fixed ministry'. For example, Müller and Craik preached in Bristol, McVicker (one of the converts of the 1859 Ulster revival) in Clapton Hall, North London, R. C. Chapman in Barnstaple, and Percy Hall in Hereford. There was thus a balance of both 'open meetings' and formal teaching or preaching.

Thus, it is not just in the twentieth century that Brethren assemblies have experienced challenges with the 'open meeting', or people started leaving because of it. This was happening all the way from the beginning.

20th Century Problems with the 'Open Meeting'

So far we have seen that the 'open meeting' is not, in itself, the problem. God's Word teaches an 'open meeting'. But we have also seen, from the Bible and from Brethren history, that if we ignore certain biblical guidelines and precautions, it can cause problems.

We come now to the main problem that is causing decline among Brethren Assemblies. Why do we have a spiritual health problem? Because, for many Brethren Assemblies, we do not have 'sound teaching', that is, healthy teaching. Some will be shocked to hear such a thing, wondering how it could be possible that, with such a rich history of great Bible teachers, this could come to pass. But consider what happened in most Brethren assemblies in the twentieth century.

Please understand that, for the next few paragraphs, I am primarily speaking about the past. Many assemblies today are no longer like the picture I will describe. But I am talking here about Brethren assemblies historically. Why? Because our autopsy report needs to work out, in the first place, why we closed over 1000 assemblies in the historical heartland of the Brethren movement (the United Kingdom) since the Second World War. What were these assemblies doing wrong?

When Brethren assemblies met on the Lord's Day, usually in the late morning, there was the Lord's Supper, and crucially, this was entirely devoted to remembrance and worship. This was the main meeting of the church, when most people were able to attend. We also usually had a Sunday School (either on Sunday afternoons, or on Sunday mornings), and then in the evening a gospel meeting. Bible teaching was left for a midweek evening or Saturday conferences.

For most Brethren assemblies, historically, there was no Bible teaching on the Lord's Day. Instead, teaching was left to other times in the week. Thus, while we might criticise other churches for having a one-man ministry, in many Brethren assemblies there was something even more problematic: no man ministry.

There might have been a short word of ministry given

after the Breaking of Bread, but this was usually brief and shallow, a mere extemporaneous devotional thought. Sometimes, not even this would happen, but instead a brother would merely 'read a passage without comment'. Rarely would there be anything that approached anything near 'feeding the flock'.

The result of this was that, on Sunday after Sunday, Christians were not given healthy food from God's Word, nor were they given the opportunity to use their gifts in teaching to benefit others, as the New Testament describes. Instead, at the Lord's Supper, anything other than the singing of hymns and prayers of thanksgiving was discouraged. In some assemblies, it was considered unspiritual even to read the Word of God at the Lord's Supper (even though singing man-made hymns was perfectly acceptable) – Bible reading was to have been done before coming out to the meeting. Due to the lack of healthy food when the assembly came together, the result would be spiritual sickness manifested in long pauses at the breaking of bread, and prayers of thanksgiving lacking in spiritual freshness and reality, so that often a brother resorted to 'tape-recording' prayers, merely repeating the same words every week.

Believers would be urged – by carrot and stick – to come out to the midweek Bible teaching meeting. But for many people, midweek meetings were difficult to attend. Mothers with young families cannot come, and some men were unable to come out because of their jobs. Those who were spiritually unhealthy would rarely ever come out – they had little desire for God's things. The result was that if half of an assembly came out to a midweek meeting it would be considered good attendance.

The midweek meeting produced an inner circle and an outer circle of fellowship in the church. The inner circle (those attending the midweek meeting) were reasonably spiritually healthy, but those in the outer circle were usually not so spiritually healthy. With little healthy Bible teaching, and with little fellowship between the two tiers of the assembly other than a brief handshake on Sunday morning after a meeting that was often unedifying, it would not take much – some personal slight or trivial disagreement – for people to leave and go to the nearest evangelical church where there was bright singing and semi-decent teaching.

Here is one of the main causes of the death of 1000 assemblies: lack of 'sound teaching', healthy feeding of God's people from His Word. Remember, too, that this problem did not just start with World War Two – many assemblies closed before this period, and probably for similar reasons. Just as good diet is essential for physical health, so it is spiritually necessary that believers get a good feed every week. But as one brother who left my home assembly and went to another church said, 'All we ever get is ice-cream'.

Three Keys: Edification, Time and Oversight

If we look at the Bible – and take it as our guide rather than human traditions or clever ideas about how to 'do church' – we notice three important differences from this 20th century Brethren 'open meeting'.

First, in the New Testament, the church came together, not simply to remember the Lord, but also for teaching. Thus, consider the three occasions in the New Testament when we read an in-depth account of the church's meeting.

- At the institution of the Lord's Supper, which is a model for our church practice, there were four chapters (John 13-16) of interactive instruction by the Lord after the bread and wine had been shared (at least five of the disciples participated in discussion during the Lord's teaching by asking questions).
- At Troas in Acts 20, the church came together for the breaking of bread, and Paul preached till midnight. This was not just a meeting for 'remembrance and worship', but also for teaching. Nor was the teaching one long sermon by Paul, for the word used (Paul 'spoke') is *dialegomai* in Greek (Acts 20:7), which means to 'converse, or dialogue'.
- In 1 Corinthians 11-14, we read about the Lord's Supper and the use of spiritual gifts in the church. Notice that in both chapters 11 and 14, we have the expression 'when you come together' (1 Cor. 11:17-20, 14:23, 26). There were not two separate meetings of the church during the week, one for remembrance and one for teaching. Instead, there was one weekly meeting of the church for both remembrance and for teaching.

In many Brethren assemblies, we have introduced an (almost) unwritten rule: at the Lord's table, we come together solely for worship and remembrance. In other words, we changed the 'open meeting' to 'open worship'. But 1 Corinthians 14:26 says: 'How is it, then, brethren? When you come together ... let all things be done for edification'. Instead of edification, we changed our motto to, 'let all things be done for remembrance and worship'. Dr. William McRae wrote this:

> In a recent issue of a Christian magazine this order of service was strongly advocated. The writer said: "In such a meeting the ministry, fellowship, and worship are centered on the Lord Jesus Christ and are under the leadership of the Holy Spirit. The introduction of evangelism or intercession is out of place. Personal testimony or experience, however soul-stirring it might be to the speaker, should be avoided unless it contributes to the contemplation of Christ. When the Lord's Supper has been observed and the worship and ministry portion has been concluded, a suitable prayer could close the meeting. At this time all necessary announcements, business reports, correspondence and other assembly affairs may be presented. While this detail is not spelled out in Scripture, it seems only fitting that we don't allow the temporal affairs of the assembly to intrude on the contemplation of our blessed Lord whom we gather together to worship. "This do in remembrance of Me."
>
> This statement shows a remarkable misunderstanding of New Testament principles. How right he is that no such detail is given in Scripture! His system is all humanly devised. I find it almost

unbelievable that one would speak of "the leadership of the Holy Spirit" in a meeting where we have spelled out what can be done, and when it can be done. Could there be a better illustration of quenching the Spirit than this?[62]

The result of this unscriptural rule ('we are just here for remembrance and worship of Christ) was that many sheep were not fed and became spiritually unwell, so that even their worship became stale and flat. We can only worship out of a heart that is full, but this requires that we are first fed from, and corrected by, God's Word. By banning healthy teaching, we also hindered worship.

In passing, it is interesting to notice that Paul does not even mention the Lord's Supper in 1 Timothy. This was not because the Lord's Supper is not important. Rather, we may assume that the Lord's Supper was so centrally important that Paul did not need to mention it – just like he did not mention the other ordinance of the church in 1 Timothy, baptism.

Please do not think that I am not arguing for getting rid of our remembrance of the Lord and replacing it with teaching. No, I am arguing that we must have both 'sound teaching' that builds up God's people, as well as worship and remembrance, and the best time to do this is when the 'whole church comes together' (1 Cor. 14:23) at the Lord's Supper.

A second difference between the 20th century Brethren 'open meeting' and the New Testament is what we might call the time factor. In Brethren assemblies, the 'open meeting' lasts for little more than 'a quiet hour', most of which is given to remembrance and worship. But when we look at the New Testament, the time for teaching and edification is much longer than a 15-minute epilogue. We see this clearly in John 13-16 and Acts 20. Paul's instructions in 1 Corinthians 14:26-40 also show that there was opportunity for many different types of contributions. Every Sunday was a conference! It was a three-course meal. No wonder the early Church, and the early Brethren, grew so quickly.

It is true that there was 'quantity control', in that the contributions were limited to 'two or three' prophets (v29) – that is, those preaching a word from the Lord that met the need of the moment, resulting in 'edification, exhortation and comfort' (1 Cor. 14:3), so that 'all may learn and all may be encouraged' (1 Cor. 14:31). But in addition to two or three messages like this, there was opportunity for discussion and input from others: 'Let two or three prophets speak, and let the others judge' (v29). The meeting was led by the Holy Spirit, not the clock on the wall. There was time, as well as freedom (within limits), for the exercise of different spiritual gifts.

A third important point to notice in the Bible was that there was 'quality control'. 'Let two or three prophets speak, and let the others judge' (1 Cor. 14:29). Just like the early Brethren quickly worked out, spiritual and gifted overseers are needed, not only to correct false teaching, but also to provide guidance and, if necessary, control, so that the time is not wasted with unprofitable talkers. This does not mean that every ungifted brother must be silenced. The elders are not a police force, but wise and loving shepherds, who are meant to patiently guide and help their flock discover their gifts and learn how to use them profitably. New believers must be encouraged to use their gifts while unhelpful contributors need to be diverted into other avenues of service. A meeting with no guidance from those who are spiritual and gifted is liable to become unprofitable. This is just as unhelpful as taking things to the other extreme: elders 'solving' the problem of unprofitable speakers by banning open participation altogether and setting up their own program. The true solution is shepherds who know their flock and speak the truth in love, for the good of all.

What about Systematic Teaching?

In the New Testament, in addition to the 'open meeting' in church, there was also systematic teaching by the apostles, particularly in the early stages of a new work. We see this happening with the apostles teaching in the temple courts in Jerusalem, with Paul and Barnabas teaching the new Christians at Antioch for a year, and in cities like Corinth and Ephesus where Paul was engaged in daily, systematic exposition of Christian truth.

Teaching by gifted preachers is an important part of church life. Consecutive expository preaching is particularly beneficial for new Christians, as it helps them to understand whole chapters and books of the Bible, showing that Scripture is coherent and relevant. Therefore, as the early Brethren also found, it is important to have systematic preaching by gifted teachers. But in the Bible this systematic instruction did not replace the 'open meeting' when the church came together – it was in addition to it. In a New Testament-style church meeting, there is room for careful exposition of the Scriptures. On the other hand, there is no reason why every meeting of the church has to be 'open'. There is room for both regular systematic, expository teaching and an 'open meeting'.

Some Brethren churches have stopped the 'open meeting' altogether in favour of systematic teaching. There are advantages to good systematic teaching, but there are also problems. First, this usually also results in the Lord's Supper being reduced to a minor and peripheral part of church life – a 10-minute slot in a service, a token perfunctory ritual. Instead of the Lord's Supper being a primary purpose of the church's gathering (Acts 20:7, 1 Cor. 11:20), often there is little depth or real feeling in the remembrance of Christ.

Second, there is more to healthy Christians than just good diet. As we saw in 1 Timothy 4, there must also be exercise and development in gift and maturity. In society, we have a problem with obesity: people eat too much and do too little exercise. We have a similar problem in the evangelical church in the Western world. If all the teaching in a church is consecutive expository preaching by a few, church turns into a spectator event that encourages pew-potatoes to sit back and enjoy the sport of sermon-tasting. The consumer convenience mentality among Christians has produced, in the words of David Wells, 'a plague of *nominal evangelicalism* which is as trite and as superficial as anything we have seen in Catholic Europe' (*The Bleeding of the Evangelical Church*[63]).

Consecutive expository preaching obeys the law of diminishing returns. New Christians benefit from expository preaching, but older mature Christians tend to stagnate in their growth; church involvement no longer drives any real spiritual development. Christians active in ministries outside the church will talk about how they are growing through serving God (e.g. in a prison Bible study), but Sunday services and midweek groups do not provide the same stimulation. This is because the way to grow spiritually is not Believe, Mature, Serve, but instead, Believe, Serve, Mature. This is precisely the way the New Testament shows us Christians growing to maturity: through using their gifts in the church meetings.

Third, while the church needs systematic instruction in the truths of God's Word, it also needs something even more important: messages from God that meet the needs of the moment. Nicely packaged, professionally delivered, three-point sermons are all very good, but preaching 35-minute expository sermons is not the only spiritual gift. Whatever happened to exhortation (Romans 12:8) or a word of wisdom? It is possible to have such perfectly planned programs that God never gets a word in. In the New Testament, it was not the pastor, or elders, or the teaching committee 'running the show', it was the Holy Spirit. The short, direct – sometimes unpolished – word from the Lord must be allowed its place in the Church.

In the New Testament, one of the keys to spiritual growth was involvement. Christianity was more than sitting and listening to sermons. That's not how learning works in secular schools or colleges today either – because people retain only 5% of lectures they hear, but 90% of what they teach. Growth requires interaction.

The key to spiritual health is not merely expository teaching in the church. The key is involvement and interaction – by people using their gifts for the benefit of others, or by sharing a testimony, or by asking questions or adding to what someone else has shared. It doesn't need to be a half-hour sermon either. It can simply be one single thought that someone has enjoyed or been challenged by. Here is William McRae again:

> Following the pattern of the New Testament church, in our Sunday evening meeting at Believers Chapel there is just such freedom [for the Spirit-led exercise of gifts]. There is always opportunity for the discovery and continuing development of spiritual gifts. Just a few weeks ago, one of the highlights of our Sunday evening meeting was when a high school lad read the first three verses of Psalm 1 and shared with us some thoughts from the Psalm. We must be very careful about our perspective. Sometimes we can become just a little resentful when we look at a young person speaking and think of him as practicing on us. Our attitude toward that situation should be like the track coach who is used to seeing men speed down the hundred-yard track in nine seconds flat, and then sits in his own living room and watches his first son take his first two or three toddling steps. ... Sometimes I leave the Sunday evening meeting almost that elated. I see a man who has become a Christian and then he

stands up and he gives out a hymn or he prays. It thrills my heart because here I see a man who is growing. He has taken his first public step and it is a sign of spiritual growth. Men talk to men about wanting to discover their spiritual gift, wondering how to discover it and how to develop it. My response is: in the meeting of the church. One major purpose of it is for the Spirit led exercise of spiritual gifts.

Martyn Lloyd-Jones, who lived through the mighty work of the Spirit of God in the Welsh revival of 1905-6 (a year-long, nation-wide 'open meeting') asked:

> Are we giving the members of the church an adequate opportunity to exercise their gifts? Are our churches corresponding to the life of the New Testament church? Or is there too much concentration in the hands of ministers and clergy? You say, "We provide opportunity for the gifts of others in week-night activities." But I still ask, Do we manifest the freedom of the New Testament church? . . . When one looks at the New Testament church and contrasts the church today, even our churches, with that church, one is appalled at the difference. ... The notion of people belonging to the church in order to come to sit down and fold their arms and listen, with just two or three doing everything, is quite foreign to the New Testament, and it seems to me it is foreign to what has always been the characteristic of the church in times of revival and of reawakening'[64].

Summary

Why should we practice the 'open meeting'? Because it is biblical, it allows development of spiritual gifts, and for God to speak through His servants. What do we need to do to make it work? We need to explain its biblical basis, to have both remembrance of Christ as well as the exercise of spiritual gifts, we need godly overseers to guide it, and we need to allow enough time for gifts to be used.

Stop relegating teaching to midweek meetings when only a fraction of people attend. On Lord's Days, have an hour of systematic teaching (if needed, including time for interactive discussion), or a Bible reading/study with a 10-minute introduction, as well as the Lord's Supper (with time for using gifts to teach and edify each other – don't have 6 or 7 hymns), separated by a break for morning tea.

This chapter has only given a brief overview of some of the issues involved. For a concise yet helpful exposition of the subject, see Dr. William McRae's booklet, *The Meeting of the Church* (Believers Chapel, Dallas), and for more in-depth treatment, see the author's book, *Do Not Quench the Spirit: a Biblical and Practical Guide to Participatory Church Gatherings*.

Some people think that the Brethren are all about getting rid of the clergy. That is not true: we are all about abolishing the laity. All God's people are meant to be serving God and growing through using our gifts.

Nor is there any reason, as we see in the case of Timothy at Ephesus, that there cannot be resident teachers working in a church to put things back on the right track again. This is the subject we turn to next.

Chapter Six

HOW TO RESUSCITATE STRUGGLING CHURCHES

In 2005, I moved to England and spent five years serving the Lord. Some time after I arrived, I approached Partnership, an agency that supports UK Brethren churches, about churches needing help. I filled in some forms with my details and Partnership put my details out to churches in their network who were looking for a full-time worker to come and help them. The very same day my details were sent out by Partnership, I was phoned at 11 pm by a brother from a church in the north of England, looking for someone to come and help them, wanting to get their church at the 'front of the queue', so to speak. I soon realised why this brother phoned so late at night. Over the next few weeks, we received about 30 requests from Brethren churches in England and Scotland asking us to come and work with them. Not because I was a spiritual superstar. I was a foreigner they knew next to nothing about. No, the reason was that many churches were desperate for help. After some time praying and investigating, we eventually spent three years working alongside an assembly in England, before we moved back to Australia.

Many Brethren assemblies are small and struggling.

They have seen no outsiders saved for many years. They are often churches with a few lovely, godly old people who are getting to the point where they cannot keep on going. If the assembly closes, much of what previous generations worked for will disappear and gospel witness in this locality might end. Closing a church is a painful and very sad business. Is there any way to turn struggling churches around?

What would the apostle Paul do? The answer is obvious: if he was unable to come himself, he would send Timothy, or Titus, or another one of his trusted co-workers, to go and spend some time there until things started to move in the right direction again. This is exactly what Timothy was left in Ephesus to do (1 Tim. 1:3), as we saw in the last chapter. Elsewhere in the New Testament, we see Timothy sent to Corinth (1 Cor. 4:17), Philippi (Phil. 2:19), and Thessalonica (1 Thess. 3:2). We also see Titus being sent by Paul to deal with troubles in Corinth (2 Cor. 7:6-7), and the churches in Crete (Titus). By the end of Paul's three-year mission in Ephesus, he had a whole group of co-workers (see Acts 19:29, 20:4) and some of them were sent on missions like this (e.g. see Colossians 4:7-10, where Paul sent Tychicus, and then later Mark to Colossae; see also Titus 3:12).

Or, if we turn from the New Testament back to the Old Testament, what does God do when the spiritual situation requires a rebuilding effort? God sends a man like Nehemiah to Jerusalem to rebuild its walls, and also its spiritual life. Or, in earlier times, God raised up prophets and send them to His people to turn them back to His ways.

The same remedy is required in many places today. If we are going to see a struggling church turned around, it is no use having a visiting team do a Holiday Bible Club once a year. Nor are visiting speakers from other churches coming to preach on Sundays going to be enough. If small and struggling churches are going to survive and thrive they need the presence, energy and gifting of a resident full-time worker.

But where, and how, are we going to find a troop of Timothys to help our struggling churches? This is a problem we desperately need to solve. We also have dropping numbers of missionaries, in line with a declining base of churches. But our responsibility remains the same: to go into all the world and preach the gospel. So how do we see new missionaries and evangelists raised up and sent out?

Here we come to the second major structural weakness that we need to address in Brethren churches: training. If the first structural weakness of Brethren churches has been teaching, then the second structural weakness of Brethren churches has been raising up new workers.

Why is training so vital in Christian ministry? Because when Christian leaders train up others around them, three things result: first, their ministry is multiplied, second, fruit is increased, and third, the impact is felt in generations to come. Christian leaders are at their best when they are raising up other leaders. There are three key steps in raising up other leaders: firstly, to spot those with potential, secondly, to invest in them, and thirdly, to entrust them with responsibility.

The importance of the next generation of full-time workers like Timothy is something that Paul touches on at the end of 1 Timothy chapter one.

Paul's Charge to Timothy

In 1 Timothy 1:18-20, Paul reminds Timothy of his calling to serve God:

> This charge I commit to you, son Timothy, according to the prophecies previously made concerning you, that by them you may wage the good warfare, having faith and a good conscience, which some having rejected, concerning the faith have suffered shipwreck, of whom are Hymenaeus and Alexander, whom I delivered to Satan that they may learn not to blaspheme (1 Tim. 1:18-20).

Paul uses three metaphors here to describe Timothy's ministry and mission.

1. Paul writes to Timothy as his 'son' – Paul is his spiritual father and mentor. He wants Timothy to know how much he loves him. He reminds Timothy of prophecies made about him, so that Timothy is conscious that it is God's will and purpose that he should continue to be involved in Christian ministry and mission. As his spiritual father, Paul encourages Timothy to follow on in the same steps, living up to Paul's example.

2. Paul describes Timothy's service as being like a soldier: 'that ... you may wage the good warfare'. In fact, the word 'charge' he uses in verse 18 is a military word and carries the idea of passing on an order from higher officers. Paul urges Timothy to 'wage the good warfare' because Christian service is a spiritual war – albeit a war that is just and good. Paul is here calling upon Timothy to 'stiffen the sinews' – he needs to be 'strong to face the foe'.
3. Then, he writes of Timothy's life as being like a sea-voyage in which others 'have suffered shipwreck' by rejecting the great truths of the faith and the warnings of conscience. Christian service is a dangerous journey, and we need to be always on the watch.

What is Paul's point here? Paul is saying this: Timothy, the baton for serving God has been handed on to you!

How Things Happened in the New Testament
In the New Testament, we see seven factors involved in the process of sending out new missionaries and ministers of the gospel. This is important to understand, because it is easy for us to get unbalanced views on this subject.

1. God raises and sends out missionaries and ministers of the gospel. We see this in Matthew 9:38, where Jesus told us to 'pray the Lord of the harvest to send out labourers into His harvest'. We also see it in Acts 13:4, where we read that Barnabas and Saul were sent out on the first missionary journey 'by the Holy Spirit'. Two verses earlier we read the Holy Spirit

saying, 'Now separate to Me Barnabas and Saul for the work to which I have called them' (Acts 13:2). It is God who sends out His servants. Christian ministry requires a divine calling. As one missionary put it, if you are not sure that God has sent you to the mission field, there will be plenty of times you will feel like going home.

2. Christians have a role to play in sending out missionaries into the harvest – we can pray for it to happen. As we have just read, Jesus has told us to pray for this (Matt. 9:38). I like prayers like this in the Bible, because we can be sure it is God's will to answer prayers like this. After all, Jesus Himself told us to pray.

3. It is not just God who sends labourers out into the harvest. Jesus and the apostles chose and called others to be their helpers. One of the first things our Lord Jesus Christ did was to choose twelve apostles and train them for three years. We see the same thing happening with the apostles and others in the book of Acts. Barnabas went and brought Saul to Antioch. Paul and Barnabas took John Mark on their first missionary journey, and Paul took Timothy on his second missionary journey. By the end of the New Testament Paul had a good-sized team of co-workers who he could send to churches that needed help.

4. Churches are also involved in the sending forth of God's servants. In Acts 13:1-4, we read about the church in Antioch: 'having fasted and prayed, and laid hands on them, they sent them [Barnabas and Saul]

away' (Acts 13:3). Actually, the word 'sent' here is literally 'released' (Gk. *apoluo*). We sometimes speak about the 'sending church' of a missionary, or even a missionary organisation that sends someone out, but this is not actually biblical language. It is God who sends labourers into His harvest. The great missionary hymn puts it this way:

> We rest on Thee, our shield and our defender!
> We go not forth alone against the foe;
> Strong in Thy strength, safe in Thy keeping tender,
> We rest on Thee, and in Thy name we go.

Nevertheless, the local church is intimately involved in the process of sending out missionaries. The local church builds up Christians to maturity and provides a place of service where Christians may grow. It is involved in praying with and giving advice to prospective missionaries, and once they are on the mission field following them with their prayers and practical support. The local church has a vital role to play.

5. There was also training involved in the New Testament. We see this most clearly with the twelve apostles who Christ called 'that they might be with Him and that He might send them out to preach' (Mk. 3:14). Christ spent three years training His disciples. The apostles also took disciples like John Mark and Timothy on their missionary journeys so that they would be assistants but also for the purpose

of training them. New Testament training was on-the-job training. But we also see Paul urging Timothy to train others in the local church, particularly in the great truths of the faith: 'the things that you have heard from me among many witnesses, commit these to faithful men who will be able to teach others also' (2 Tim. 2:2).

6. There must also have been an inclination and ability on the part of those who were involved in serving God. Those who were called as disciples (i.e. trainees), either by the Lord or His apostles, must have had some desire to serve God. Very few people have ever been missionaries who refused to do the job. Even Jonah had to learn – the hard way – to follow God's call. In addition to this, we know from the New Testament letters that people who were involved in serving God were gifted by Him for this ministry: 'He Himself gave some to be apostles, some prophets, some evangelists, and some pastors and teachers' (Eph. 4:11). The Lord does not call people to serve Him who do not have the gifts for it.

7. Lastly, it is surely true that certain means were used by God to encourage prospective missionaries and disciples. When Paul and Barnabas returned from their first missionary journey, they not only reported on what God had done in their own home church at Antioch (Acts 14:27), but also at various churches (Acts 15:3) on their way to Jerusalem where they also reported at the council meeting (Acts 15:4, 12). We are told that such reports caused great joy (15:3), and

there is no doubt that missionary reports of God at work today (whether at missionary conferences, or by missionary letters, or reports in magazines) are used by God to stir up the hearts of some people to become missionaries.

Here is the vital point to notice: there are more factors involved than simply the divine call. This, as we will see, is where many Brethren assemblies have a weakness.

Training in Brethren Assemblies

Let us now compare how God raised up full-time workers in the New Testament, with how we do it in Brethren assemblies. Here we will see five problems that add up to a structural weakness.

Firstly, whereas in the New Testament multiple factors were involved in people going into full-time ministry, in Brethren assemblies the impression was sometimes given that going into full-time ministry was the result of a mysterious divine call alone, and without any of the other human factors at all.

In particular, the first great problem in Brethren assemblies has been the neglect by full-time workers to take on apprentices (or disciples, trainees) like we read the Lord doing in the gospels, and His apostles in the Book of Acts. I speak as someone who is guilty in this matter. It is only now in my middle-age that I am on the active look-out for gifted young men and women who I can encourage to get involved in serving God full-time.

Instead of waiting for others to put themselves forward for full-time ministry, the apostles deliberately 'headhunted' gifted younger brethren who they asked to accompany them in their service for God. The Lord and His apostles multiplied Christian ministry through training new disciples. This was the primary human means by which new people were involved in full-time ministry in the New Testament – by invitation. Yet among Brethren assemblies, instead of seeking to multiply their ministry through apprentices, full-time ministers have tended to reinforce the idea that a divine call to full-time service is a mysterious process. How have they reinforced this idea? By never inviting any apprentices to come along with them, or training up others to do what they do. While this is not true everywhere (for example, in days gone by, evangelists would take on younger men to help them), yet in some places, full-time workers have been negligent in this area of discipling others to take on the same role as themselves.

A second problem with getting people involved in full-time service stems from the fact that Brethren assemblies do not believe in a clergy-laity division. As a result, we have tended to be uncomfortable with the idea of a full-time teacher in a particular church. As we saw, however, some of the early Brethren leaders, like Müller and Chapman, filled this role. This did not mean that they did all the teaching or were the only ones who were able to use their gifts. However, the early Brethren were happy to allow their most gifted leaders to exercise their gift to the full, and the result was the building up of the work.

It is perfectly possible for a full-time worker to come and help an assembly for some time without becoming a one-man ministry team. We have seen in the previous chapter that Timothy came to Ephesus and worked there without becoming 'the first Bishop of Ephesus', or 'Senior Pastor Tim' (as some Bible notes and commentators suggest). Nor did Timothy do all the teaching – there was still open opportunity for others to use their gifts as well. It is possible, and biblical, for people today to fill the same role as Timothy did in Ephesus.

A third problem in Brethren assemblies is that, despite claiming that in Brethren assemblies we have no clergy-laity division, nevertheless we have given some evangelists and missionaries an exalted, almost super-human, status.

Let me put it this way. When my great-uncle T. E. Wilson went to Angola as a missionary, he was only 21 years old. Similarly, my grandfather, William Bunting, went into full-time evangelistic work at 21 years of age. Both men had been involved in evangelistic outreach in Northern Ireland and had finished apprenticeships, one as a carpenter in Harland and Wolff Shipyards, the other as a draper. Later in life, after they had spent many years studying and teaching and preaching the Bible, both men were considered exceptional Bible teachers, but it would probably be fair to say that they were not exceptional Bible teachers or gospel preachers at 21 years of age.

People involved in Christian training nowadays like to say that there are three Cs they are looking to develop in new recruits: character, convictions and competency[65]. But the most important of these is character – not competency (gifting). What matters most is that a new trainee fears God, is full of zeal for the Lord and love for others, and is humble and obedient to God's Word.

Gift takes time to come to full maturity. Just look at Timothy. Paul had to write to him twice about his gift. First, he writes, 'Do not neglect the gift that is in you, which was given to you by prophecy with the laying on of the hands of the eldership' (1 Tim. 4:14). Then in 2 Timothy 1:6, Paul says, 'I remind you to stir up the gift of God which is in you through the laying on of my hands'.

In the New Testament, the Lord Jesus called twelve men to be his disciples and apostles, but none of them showed any exceptional gift or ability at the beginning. They were very ordinary men. The Lord transformed them into great men of God, and it did not happen overnight, and they made mistakes along the way.

The point is this: we often set the bar too high in our evaluation of possible or prospective full-time workers. If they are not exceptional preachers, we dismiss them as not ready to serve God. This is a mistake and a problem.

The fourth problem is related: we do not provide a pathway for people to move into full-time ministry. Think of it this way: Brethren assemblies have historically tended to have four types of full-time workers. First were overseas missionaries – people of great faith and courage. Next came evangelists who travelled the home country preaching the gospel. Thirdly, there were itinerant Bible teachers, who tended to be older, retired brethren. Then, fourthly, more recently, there were people involved in service ministries, like printing or camp administration.

It is not untrue to say that some of these full-time workers were revered – particularly missionaries and great evangelists. One well-known itinerant Bible teacher said to one member of my family, speaking about a missionary, that 'people worship the ground he walks on'. I have also heard one family member say about my grandfather the evangelist in Northern Ireland, that some people treated him like an Old Testament prophet. Now, if I may paraphrase the words of Moses, 'would that all our full-time workers were men of the calibre of Old Testament prophets' (see Num. 11:29). Nor do I have any problem with people showing respect to missionaries who have sacrificed not only the comforts of home, but also their health and safety, to take the gospel to unreached people of the world. God will greatly reward these men and women of God, and we do well to honour them.

But my point here is simply this. Growing up in the assemblies, it almost seemed as if there was such a great gulf fixed between these great men (and women) of faith and ordinary Christians that it was the height of sinful ambition for any lesser saints to think that they might ever be like them and serve God in any full-time capacity. It was as ridiculous as thinking that God might call you to be an Old Testament prophet. Even if you were a spiritual and active believer serving God, unless you felt called to be an overseas missionary, the idea of being involved in full-time ministry was as unlikely and incomprehensible as visiting the moon.

There was no pathway between the ordinary Christian service of normal believers and the super-exalted status of some full-time workers. Full-time ministry was not something that anybody thought themselves worthy of, because full-time Christian work was equated with being a super-spiritual missionary or evangelist hero.

The result was that it did not enter the heads of young Christians to think about serving God in a full-time capacity. They were never encouraged to think of it – except possibly as overseas missionaries. They simply devoted themselves to secular studies and training so they could get a good career, then settle down and have a family.

A fifth and final problem in Brethren assemblies relates to training within assemblies. By this I mean the sort of training that Paul told Timothy to do in 2 Timothy 2:2 – that is, identify a group of faithful men and instruct them in the truths Timothy had heard from Paul, so they could teach others. Here, we are not talking about training for full-time service; simply training in Bible truth and teaching. Younger brethren have traditionally been given the opportunity to exercise their gift by preaching a few times a year. But high-quality preaching requires more than this: either a lifetime of full-time ministry, or intensive training.

The problem is that this sort of training was not something that happened very often in Brethren assemblies. Yes, there was usually a Bible class for young Christians, but this was basic Christian teaching rather than advanced instruction. Again, please notice from the Bible that this training was something a resident full-time worker – i.e. Timothy – was told to do. But there is no reason elders could not do it, using resources like the author's *Believers Bible Doctrine Handbook* and *Believers*

Preaching Handbook. By training up others to teach the truths of God's Word, Timothy could move on to help other churches or reach out with the gospel in new areas.

Training within our assemblies – in understanding doctrine more deeply, in training how to preach better, in preparing a new generation of elders – is something that has been neglected.

In fact, when Brethren assemblies were at their height, there were so many good visiting Bible teachers that could be invited to preach that there was hardly any opportunity for younger men to exercise their gifts at all. There is a story told in English assemblies about young men who were told to 'sit and listen, sit and listen, sit and listen', and when they were old men, all they could do was 'sit and listen'.

G. H. Lang said, in relation to preaching, that 'the way to do it is to do it'. In other words, you got better at preaching the more you did it. This is why missionaries came back from the field far better preachers and teachers than when they left their home country. Preaching once or twice a year will not develop the gift of a man, any more than playing golf once or twice a year will improve anyone's score. We have failed to intensively train younger generations.

How to Improve our Training

Having compared how training happened in the New Testament with how training has tended (not) to happen in Brethren assemblies, let us now turn and look at some other modern training methods outside our Brethren assemblies. Training is one important reason why some other evangelical churches are not declining, while Brethren assemblies are. Please understand that I am not suggesting that we should just imitate what other churches do. I want to be very clear here: what many other churches do is not biblical, particularly the process by which they ordain their clergy. But, nevertheless, we will look at two training schemes here, and try to see why they have been successful.

The first training scheme I want to mention is called MTS, which stands for Ministry Training Strategy. It is a training scheme run in Australia for evangelicals. Colin Marshall (who was in charge of MTS) writes, "After the gospel itself, the greatest need of the Christian church is to keep finding and training people who will faithfully teach the Bible to both Christians and non-Christians"[66].

MTS is a two-year, full-time apprenticeship based within a church or a specialist ministry team (e.g. university outreach). It is based upon a relationship between an apprentice and a MTS trainer – an older and more experienced Christian leader who mentors the trainee. It involves two years of prayer, Bible study and Christian service. The purpose of MTS is to give people the opportunity to see what it is really like being a 'full-time' gospel worker.

Why a two-year, full-time training course? MTS argues its case as follows: if someone wishes to become a farmer, they do not go off to agricultural college and learn about farming – they work on a farm, harvesting in the heat of summer, and out at night in the cold of winter. In this way, they get a true picture of what farming involves, and can decide if this is the right course. In the same way, the best preparation for full-time ministry is as an apprentice being mentored by another leader.

Someone might suggest that a person wishing to train in Christian ministry should work part-time to support themselves. However, if a trainee is doing half a week of ministry (evangelism, discipleship, teaching) as well as working part-time, they will have little time left for serious Bible study, which is necessary for their spiritual growth, as well as for preparation for ministry. This is a recipe for burn-out, not a true reflection of full-time ministry. Gospel workers who do not put a priority on their own relationship with God, nor put in the time for in-depth Bible study, are going to be dangerously ill-equipped for serving God. Their own spiritual lives will be impoverished, and they will be superficial and shallow in their teaching and sharing of God's Word with others. The apostle Paul spent 14 years of private preparation before embarking on ministry (see Galatians 1 and 2), while the Lord's apostles spent three years of full-time apprenticeship before ministry.

Over the last 40 years, MTS has had more than 4000 people go through this program. Think about it from the perspective of most evangelical denominations. Every single one of their churches must have an ordained minister. That means that they cannot afford NOT to be training up new people to fill the shoes of older ministers who are retiring. Not everyone who does MTS goes into an ordained ministry role afterwards, but it provides excellent training in serving God regardless. More importantly, it provides a pathway, a first step, for someone interested in serving God, to see if it might be what God is calling them to.

The second training program is one that operates in England, the Cornhill Training course, although it has now been exported all over the world. Cornhill is a two-year part-time preaching training course. It aims to have trainees preaching 16 times over these two years in a practice situation where they get feedback and training, and so improve in their preaching, as well as providing some theological studies.

I ran across the Cornhill Training course in England because a nearby Baptist church hired a graduate from the course as their Assistant Minister. The situation in three Baptist churches in the area near where we lived was this: they were struggling to find people to be their ministers. As a result, they were going through what they called an 'interregnum'. They were on the lookout for a new minister – but no one was available or suitable. This is a problem that is being faced by more and more small to medium sized evangelical churches today.

Why are evangelical churches struggling to find ministers? Here are some reasons:

- burn-out rates for ministers are high (maybe because it is an unbiblical expectation for one person to do all the ministry and handle all the pastoral problems for an entire church?)
- formal theological education is unappealing to many people, because it is very expensive, takes a long time,

may involve moving your whole family to live in another place, and not everyone is academically inclined. Therefore, fewer people with the required theological degrees are available for Baptist churches.

The solution that many evangelical churches were adopting in England was therefore to hire someone who had done the Cornhill preaching training course. This course had another advantage over formal theological training. Theological graduates often leave Bible college with a love for discussing deep theological questions, but their preaching is as dull as ditchwater. Cornhill trainees, by contrast, were prepared to do the most important task in Christian ministry – preach the Bible faithfully in a way that actually connects with ordinary people.

Both of these training courses, MTS and Cornhill, were intensely practical, rather than academic. They were apprenticeships rather than tertiary education. This is why they are extremely popular and effective. This apprentice-style training is what we see the Lord Jesus and the apostles doing in the New Testament – providing on-the-job training. Both of these training courses were mentored training – rather than classroom lectures – just like the Lord and His apostles did when training others. Both of these courses were suitable for anyone – even someone who wanted to teach Sunday School as their main ministry for the Lord. Lastly, both of these training courses provide a model for Brethren full-time workers to train up others, because they can be done in any location, without any institution or fancy acronym, whether in conjunction with an existing assembly or in some other outreach situation. All it requires is a full-time worker who is willing to train and mentor an apprentice in preaching and gospel witness. How would this work out in practice?

Assembly Apprentices

We need to encourage younger generations of Christians to develop their gifts and grow through serving God and studying His Word. We want to encourage some of them to think about serving God full-time. We need to provide a pathway and opportunities for young people keen to serve God, whether they end up working in full-time ministry or not, so that the Lord's work is the focus of their lives (rather than career, relationships, material blessings, leisure, etc). We must either use the next generation or lose struggling churches. In fact, we must either use the next generation or lose the next generation – because there will not be Brethren assemblies left for them to belong to.

Here are four questions that need to be thought through in relation to a two-year, full-time apprentice training program. Apprentices who are working with a missionary or evangelist would usually be working alongside them every day of the week, but the following questions and answers refer to an apprentice working in or alongside an assembly, with mentoring from a full-time worker (or retired missionary) who is only able to visit occasionally.

1. **What Gospel Work would Trainees be Doing?**
Depending on the particular ministry situation they

choose to focus on, trainees could be involved in evangelistic bible studies, street evangelism, discipleship studies with new Christians, leading small group Bible studies, personal evangelism on university campuses, preaching, running camps for kids and youth, running midweek kids clubs, running youth groups, and other outreach work.

2. **What mentoring would be involved?** Trainees would have a weekly meeting with a mentor (either in person or by phone or over the internet) for prayer, as well as discussion of passages of Scripture being studied and read, or meetings being taken and teaching happening. In this way, the trainee would be given sound advice on practical and biblical issues. In addition, mentors would need to focus on training apprentices in teaching God's Word to others, because teaching God's Word to others faithfully and relevantly is the most important job of someone in Christian ministry. This would involve getting trainees to preach up to ten times a year (in church, or in private, or over the internet), receiving feedback and coaching, as well as giving instruction on important elements of preaching. The apprentice would also meet weekly with one or more of the elders of the local assembly (if they are doing the training in an assembly) for prayer and planning of the work of the assembly, again providing pastoral support, advice and encouragement.

3. **What Bible Study Would a Trainee Do?** The most important part of any discipleship training is growing in one's own relationship with the Lord. This means establishing the discipline of getting up early every day to spend quality time with the Lord. Meditating on God's Word and praying is by far the most important part of the trainee's day. This would be the first priority discussed each week with a mentor. In addition to this, there are several other important areas of Bible study that the mentor would oversee:

- Getting a broad knowledge of Scripture by reading through the entire Bible in a year and discussing this with a mentor.
- Getting an in-depth knowledge of Scripture: trainees would be encouraged to become an expert in two or three New Testament books per year - Romans, Galatians, and James (first year), 1 Corinthians, Ephesians, 1 Timothy (second year)
- Trainees would also need to be encouraged to start thinking about doctrinal and practical Christian issues. The mentor would need to give the trainee some reading, and have discussions about these subjects.

The trainee would be expected to spend two mornings and one whole day in study every week, setting a pattern of lifelong Bible study. Mentors would oversee this study.

4. **How would trainees be financially supported?** The old saying, 'you might as well start as you intend to go on' applies here, and I think disciples of Christ can hardly do better than live like the Master did. 'Living by faith', like most assembly full-time workers, is not easy, and teaches important lessons all by itself, in humbling us and making us totally dependent upon God. But the Scripture also teaches that churches have financial responsibilities to those who are working for God in them (1 Tim. 5:17), and surely, with all the millions of dollars in buildings the Brethren have sold off during the last fifty years, some could be ploughed back into the most important investment we can make – into training our young people who want to serve God.

Conclusion

We need to be sending out missionaries to take the message of Christ overseas. We also need new full-time gospel workers to take the message of Christ to our home countries, and to plant new churches. We also need new full-time gospel workers to come and help small and struggling assemblies so that they start to grow again by gospel outreach and Bible teaching. This means that we need to get busy training new workers. The main responsibility for doing this lies with existing missionaries, evangelists and full-time workers. But all believers can pray that the Lord will send out labourers into His harvest.

Chapter Seven

THE SOURCE OF THE POWER

In a previous chapter, I told the story of the 1859 revival that started in Ulster and spread throughout the United Kingdom. But across the Atlantic at the same time, something very similar happened.

In 1857, Jeremiah Lanphier, a middle-aged businessman, was hired by Old Dutch North Church to do visitation work in New York. The inner-city church was dwindling in numbers, and while other churches were closing, the trustees decided on a last-ditch plan. For three months Lanphier visited boarding houses and businesses, inviting people to the church, to little avail.

Then, on September 23, he decided to hold a weekly lunchtime prayer meeting for businessmen. He distributed advertising leaflets for the meeting, and placed a sign outside inviting people to come, but at 12 noon when the meeting was supposed to start, no one turned up. At 12:10 still no one had come. Lanphier started praying on his own, and it was not until 12:30 that he heard the stairs creak as one man came in. By the end of the meeting, six men had joined him. They decided to hold another prayer meeting the next week. This time, twenty men came to pray, and the week after, forty. Lanphier decided to hold his prayer meeting every day.

That very week, the United States experienced its worst ever financial crash. For twenty years, the country had been enjoying unprecedented economic prosperity, with western states opening up, a gold rush and a railroad building boom. People were too busy making money to worry about God. But three weeks after Lanphier started his prayer meeting, on October 10, 1857, the great stock market crash occurred: banks failed, people instantly lost everything, jobs disappeared, and families went hungry.

Within a short time, 3000 people were attending Lanphier's prayer meeting. By January 1858, there were twenty daily prayer meetings in New York, and newspapers reporting on them. Within six months 10,000 businessmen were meeting daily for prayer. More importantly, as a result of the prayer meetings there were many conversions. Prayer meetings spread to many other places, and revival swept the country. In Philadelphia, where 150,000 attended prayer meetings in four months, it is estimated there were 10,000 conversions in 1858. When the revival was at its peak, it is estimated there were 50,000 conversions a week. Some say there were up to one million converts in the USA in total.

In this chapter, we are going to look again at prayer. Spurgeon once offered to show some Sunday visitors to his Tabernacle in London the heating plant for the building. The puzzled visitors followed him downstairs to a room where Spurgeon showed them hundreds gathered praying. He said: here is the source of our power.

Paul wrote, 'For the weapons of our warfare are not carnal (that is, human ability, cleverness, and organization) but mighty (or, ***powerful***) ***in God*** for pulling down strongholds, casting down arguments and every high thing that exalts itself against the knowledge of God, bringing every thought into captivity to the obedience of Christ, (2 Cor. 10:4-5)

E. M. Bounds, the great man of prayer said this: 'What the church needs today is not more machinery or better, not new organizations or more and novel methods, but men whom the Holy Ghost can use – men of prayer, men mighty in prayer. The Holy Ghost does not flow through methods, but through men. He does not come on machinery but on men. He does not anoint plans, but men – men of prayer'. We are going to look at three more lessons about prayer in 1 Timothy 2.

Why We Should Pray

In verse 1, Paul says, 'Therefore I exhort first of all that supplications, prayers, intercessions and giving of thanks be made for all men'.

Notice: prayer is a first priority in the church. Is that true of your church? You can tell whether it is by how many people are coming out to pray, how many answers to prayer you are seeing, and significantly, by how many people are being saved through your church.

Why is prayer of first importance? Because of the gospel message. We see this in verses 2 to 6. Paul gives an outline of the gospel here. 'God our Saviour desires all men to be saved and to come to the knowledge of the truth' (v3). And what is the truth? 'There is one God and one mediator between God and men, the man Christ

Jesus who gave Himself a ransom for all – to be testified in due time' (v5). So why is prayer of first priority? Because of the gospel.

Paul urges us in verse 1 to pray for all men. Do we care that people around us are perishing? Well, let us pray for their salvation.

Then in verse 2 Paul urges us to pray for the government, so that we will have conditions of peace and freedom. Why do we want this? So our business booms? So we can go on nice holidays? No, so that the gospel can spread without government interference or restrictions.

The great man of God Hudson Taylor, who went to China as a missionary in the 1800s, depending on God for financial support without asking for money from men, also realised that it is only by prayer, by calling upon God in faith, that the gospel spreads. He once wrote to a missionary hoping to evangelise a whole Chinese province with these words: 'If you are going to take that province, you will have to advance on your knees'.

We must be people of prayer. We need churches that are known for their prayer meetings. That is where the spiritual power comes from, and results in blessing.

I know of an assembly in a small town in Scotland in the 1980s that was down to one old man and two old women. But instead of giving up, they started praying, and God sent them a family with four children, and then others, and God's work in that Scottish village revived and still 40 years later it is carried on. It does not matter how low things get – how small or weak or bleak the situation is. God promises that if His people humble themselves, he will hear their prayer from heaven, and answer. God's power is sufficient to revive His work, if we are prepared to humble ourselves and pray to Him. Do we believe this, or do we think God doesn't keep His promises?

How We Should Pray

Twice in this chapter, we are given advice on how to pray. In verse 1, we are told about the ways in which we can pray, then in verse 9 we are given conditions for prayer: how not to pray.

How should we pray? In verse 1, Paul writes, 'Therefore I exhort first of all that supplications, prayers, intercessions, and giving of thanks be made for all men'.

Why does Paul use four different words for prayer here? Because there are different types of prayers. The word supplications has the idea of begging, and it comes from a Greek word meaning 'needs'. Here is the most basic sort of prayer – there are things I desperately need, and I ask God for them. In this first sort of prayer, we are looking at our situation, and at our problems. By the way, the Hebrew word for 'supplications' used in the Old Testament means 'favours'. We can ask God for favours, because He is a gracious, giving God.

The second word, prayers, focuses our attention not so much on ourselves and our needs, but on God who is great enough to answer them. Here we are taking our eyes off our problems, and looking to God as the solution.

John Newton, the ex-slave trader, preacher and hymnwriter put it like this: Thou art coming to a king, large petitions with thee bring, for His love and power and such, none can ever ask too much.

Every now and then in our churches we face problems, and our temptation often is to resort to 'political' solutions to fix them. People complain and grumble, or agitate and argue, and sometimes even fight, to get what they want. The result is often quite ungodly behaviour, and sometimes even church splits. But the solution to all our problems is God, and we need to seek His face in earnest prayer – not politics – until He provides the answer.

The third word 'intercessions' teaches us that we should pray for others too. Here we are not looking at our problems, but around at others.

Then the fourth word used is thanksgivings. Here we are looking backward at all the ways God has answered prayer in the past and been gracious to us, and as we do this, we are filled with joy and hope because we can trust God to answer prayer in the future. Oftentimes we see David in the Psalms pouring out his troubles, but he finishes by praising God for what He is going to do. This is true prayer – when we get our eyes on the Lord.

I know an elderly missionary who was fond of saying, 'praying is working'. I think this old missionary was right. Prayer is not a peripheral or preliminary part of God's works: it is the primary part of God's work.

Let's get very practical about how we should pray. In the church where I am a member, we have seen God's blessing in a special way in this past year. What is the secret? I am convinced it is largely the result of prayer. I mentioned earlier about some of the special prayer meetings we had over the Christmas period this past year, and the blessing that followed.

But what about our normal prayer life as a church? How do we go about praying? First, we have an assembly prayer meeting on Tuesday evenings. In addition, we have an early morning prayer meeting on Fridays where half a dozen men gather to pray. We also have a prayer meeting before our Sunday services. Then there is a ladies' Bible study on Tuesday mornings where there is, again, a time of prayer for the work of God. Then we have mini-prayer meetings before some of the church's outreaches – before the café, and during our midweek children's outreach. Additionally, we also have half a dozen individuals who meet up during the week with other believers to pray in pairs or in small groups. Finally, there is prayer at family devotions. This is important – family prayers are a key feature of past revivals. If you want to see God working, switch off the TV, and have family prayers.

Not everyone is able to get out to a midweek evening prayer meeting. Some mothers with young children need to stay home and some fathers have to get up early for work, and some elderly believers do not want to drive on country roads after dark. But we try and encourage everyone in the church to find times to meet together to pray as God's people.

Why? Because the amount of prayer matters. James 5:16 says that 'the fervent prayer of a righteous man has much power'. If we are casual and careless about prayer, God is not going to take our prayer seriously. We sometimes wonder what Paul meant when he said, 'Pray without ceasing' (1 Thess. 5:17). But in times of revival, this is exactly what is happening – unceasing prayer. The secret to seeing blessing in a church is not elaborate planning, eloquent preaching, or educated professors, it is exceptional praying. George Müller said this: 'More prayer, more exercise of faith, more patient waiting, and the result will be blessing'.

But it is not just the number of prayer meetings that a church has or the numbers of people praying that counts – it is also how we pray. This is what Paul writes about in verse 8, where he gives more guidance about how we should pray, or more particularly, how we should not pray.

Paul says, 'I desire therefore that the men pray everywhere, lifting up holy hands, without wrath and doubting' (v8). Paul gives three conditions for answered prayer: holiness, love and faith.

God wants us to be holy people: we need to be lifting up holy hands in prayer. Holiness involves separation from sin. In Psalm 66:18 we are told, 'If I regard iniquity in my heart, the Lord will not hear'. James says in 5:16 that the fervent prayer of a righteous man avails much (or has much power). But holiness also here involves being people who are devoted to God, not being people whose minds are filled with the things of the world. We need to be living consecrated lives, surrendered to the Lord. God cannot have fellowship with sin or unholiness or worldliness.

Secondly, we read that prayer must be without wrath. We must not be angry with others. We must not be holding a grudge, or an unforgiving spirit. In Mark 11:25-26 the Lord said 'whenever you stand praying, if you have anything against anyone, forgive him, that your Father in heaven may also forgive you your trespasses. But if you do not forgive, neither will your Father in heaven forgive your trespasses'.

Thirdly, we need to pray without doubting. We need to pray in faith. The Lord said, 'Have faith in God. For assuredly, I say to you, whoever says to this mountain, Be removed and be cast into the sea, and does not doubt in his heart, but believes that those things he says will be done, he will have whatever he says. Therefore I say to you, whatever things you ask when you pray, believe that you receive them, and you will have them' (Mk. 11:22-24). It is pointless praying unless we believe.

Believing prayer was one of the characteristics of the 1857 revival in New York. Once God started working through the prayer meetings at Fulton Street, and particularly as people started to get saved, the faith of people grew and they started believing that God would answer their prayers. So they started praying for particular people to be saved. They would pass slips of paper up the front to the chairman with names of people to be prayed for and other specific requests for prayer. In a church in the Midwest twenty-five women started praying once a week for their unsaved husbands. Their pastor later travelled to New York to tell the Fulton Street prayer meeting that all twenty-five had now been converted.

Believing prayer characterized the Ulster revival too. One of the four young men who formed the first prayer meeting in 1857 was reading the *Narrative of Some of the Lord's Dealings with George Müller*. The account of how

God had provided for the orphans convinced him that the Lord hears and answers prayer. So he and his friends started praying, and then started seeing people converted. But when news came of the revival in the United States, they asked each other, 'Why may we not have such a blessed work here, seeing that God did such things for Mr. Müller simply in answer to prayer?'[67] They started to pray bigger prayers and they started to organize public prayer meetings, like in the US. And revival came.

This is one of the characteristics of prayer in the church where I am a member. At our midweek prayer meeting, we firstly spend some time discussing specific people or needs for prayer. Then, instead of vague and eloquent prayers that go all around the world without asking for anything specific, we pray for these needs.

What are the characteristics of believing prayer? Believing prayer is earnest, sacrificial, specific, expectant, and persistent. Prayer like this leads to revival.

Our Lord urged us to ask for big things in prayer:

> Most assuredly, I say to you, he who believes in Me, the works that I do he will do also, and greater works than these he will do, because I go to My Father. And whatever you ask in My name, that I will do, that the Father may be glorified in the Son. If you ask anything in My name, I will do it. (John 14:12-14)

Who Should Pray

Finally, in verses 8 to 15, Paul speaks about who should pray. Here we come to an issue that has caused some tension in Brethren assemblies over the years: different gender roles in the church.

Nathan Smith, in his book *Roots, Renewal and the Brethren*, gives the interview reports of people who have left assemblies in the USA, and a number of interviewees listed the 'marginalization of women' as one reason. It would therefore not be right for us to ignore what Paul says here in 1 Timothy 2 about gender roles in the church.

Paul says in verse 8 that he desires the men to pray everywhere, and the word he uses he is gender specific: it is the males who should pray everywhere (literally: in every place). By contrast in verses 11 and 12 he says that a woman is to learn in silence with all submission, and in verse 12 he says, "I do not permit a woman to teach or to have authority over a man, but to be in silence'. What Paul is doing here is transitioning from the subject of prayer, using it as a launch pad to talk about different gender roles in the church.

These are controversial issues today, but we can all agree our Western culture is in uproar over this matter of gender. Recently, a US supreme court judge was not prepared to give a definition of the word 'woman', despite being nominated for the job because she was a woman. We have transgender people changing from men into women (or vice versa), and before that, we had debates over homosexuality and gay marriage. And before that, we had the feminist revolution.

The different flanks of the gender movement are now turning on each other. Just think about what happens when a lady in a lesbian relationship decides to transition to become a man: her partner can no longer call herself a lesbian, so what is she? Feminists and transgender advocates are at each other's throats, because transgenderism undermines feminism if it is possible for biological men to claim the same distinctive rights that feminists say are reserved solely for women. It is not a little ironic that the feminist claim that men and women are equal is now undermining feminism itself.

Despite the cultural confusion, the biological facts about gender are very clear: men and women are different, in at least ten important ways:

1. men are physically stronger and faster than women. Numerous scientific studies have shown this[68], but at a more obvious level, in 2016 in Australia, an under-15 boys' football club team (the Newcastle Jets) beat the Australian national women's soccer team (the Matildas), and the score was 7-0. In 2017, the women's fastest 100 metres time in the world (10.78 seconds by US runner Tori Bowie) was beaten by over 125 boys (and 15,000 men) in competition,
2. men and women are different genetically: in every cell of the human body, women have two X chromosomes, but men have an X and a Y chromosome – and these can't be changed,
3. only women can give birth,
4. men and women are anatomically different – they have different reproductive organs,
5. men and women are 'wired' differently: men tend to be interested in fixing things, while women prefer to help and care for people. The result is that men and

women make different career choices: in Sweden (which has had freedom of career choice for 50 years), 90% of engineers are men and 90% of nurses are women.
6. men are more aggressive. The result is that 90% of prisoners in jail are men.
7. Women are emotionally different to men, and tend to have higher levels of anxiety and emotional pain.
8. Women are also more compassionate and agreeable.
9. even intellectually, men and women are different: 98% of chess grandmasters are men, because men have a greater range of intelligence – men are smarter (and dumber) than women. Another way of saying this is that women are more balanced.
10. Women are more beautiful.

Men and women are equal in important ways – both are made in the image of God (Genesis 1:26), but they are also different, because they were designed by God to complement each other by fulfilling different roles.

This is what the Bible teaches in different places, and what Paul argues in this passage. In verses 9-10, he speaks about women's appearance. Paul says 'in like manner also, that the women adorn themselves in modest apparel, with propriety and moderation, not with braided hair or gold or pearls or costly clothing, but, which is proper for women professing godliness, with good works'. Christian women are told to dress modestly, and warned against drawing attention to their appearance with jewellery, fancy hairdos or expensive dresses. Why? Because, says God, Christian women are to be attractive by their godliness and good works.

Then in verses 11 and 12, Paul speaks about women in church. He says, 'I do not permit a woman to teach or to have authority over a man, but to be in silence'. Paul prohibits three things: (a) women publicly teaching in the church, (b) women leading in the church (because Paul is about to deal with the subject of church leadership in the next chapter, 1 Timothy 3), and (c) women publicly speaking in the church, which appears to include praying – verse 8 tells the men to pray.

Now, I take it that these verses are limited to church situations, for two reasons. Firstly, because 1 Timothy is all about how we ought to conduct ourselves in the church (as 1 Tim. 3:15 says), and secondly because the expression 'in every place' in v8 is a similar expression Paul uses in Titus 1 when he is talking about the churches where he tells Titus to appoint elders 'in every city' (see also Acts 15:36). These verses are speaking about church life: men should pray publicly in the church and women are to be silent. There are other situations outside of church where these prohibitions do not apply.

In verses 13 and 14 Paul gives two reasons for his teaching about women. First because of the created order: Adam was created first. Then secondly, because of the fall: the woman was deceived. This does not mean that women should not teach because they are more gullible or unintelligent, and more likely to be teaching error. The point is that Satan turned God's order upside down by approaching Eve, in effect urging her to take the lead in disobedience. Satan's desire is to subvert the Divine order, and he wants others to follow His rebellion against authority. This is why Paul mentions a woman's submission in v11 and authority in v12 – God has established an order and He has placed man in the position of authority, not the woman. Speaking in church assumes a position of authority by saying things publicly, which Paul says is not the woman's place. In v15, he says that the woman's role is primarily in the family – bringing up godly children who are characterised by faith, love, holiness and self-control.

God has important work for women to do. He has given women spiritual gifts to use. Women are not just here to make cakes and cut sandwiches for church functions. We read of women who were Paul's co-workers in spreading the gospel (in many countries women can go where a man cannot; even in the West it is not right for an evangelist to meet with a woman privately). We read of women who taught and instructed other believers, and in New Testament times there were prophetesses who brought God's message to people. But for a mother of children, the woman's primary sphere of service is in the family. Someone put it like this: the most important converts you will ever see saved are your own children.

In summary, then, why does Paul talk about gender in 1 Timothy 2:8-15? Because God made men and women different, and He wants the men to stand up and be spiritual leaders, both in the church and the family.

Objections, Omissions and Apparent Contradictions
Women's roles has been one of the most contentious

issues in Brethren assemblies – people have left over it. Many evangelical churches now have women pastors and preachers, and reject what I have said about women's silence. Indeed, the majority of evangelical scholarship today argues for women speaking in church in some way or another. They point to the apparent contradiction between Paul's prohibitions on women speaking in church (1 Timothy 2, 1 Corinthians 14) and his mention of women praying and prophesying without any hint of censure in 1 Corinthians 11:5. They suggest that this apparent contradiction is best solved by a compromise position. Thus, Brethren writer F. F. Bruce argued for an apparent contradiction by saying (commenting on 1 Corinthians 11:5), 'That there was liberty in the church (for it is church order, not private or domestic devotion, that is in view here) for women to pray or prophesy is necessarily implied by Paul's argument'[69]. Bruce went on to express discomfort with Paul's words in 1 Corinthians 14:34-35 (where women are told to 'keep silent in the church, for they are not permitted to speak ... for it is shameful for women to speak in church') by saying, 'After the recognition in 11:5ff of women's authority to pray and prophesy, the imposition of silence on them here is strange'[70].

Faced with a stand-off between these two passages, many evangelicals today opt to interpret Paul's words in 1 Corinthians 14:34-35 as less than a total prohibition. Some argue that the word 'speak' means to 'chatter' in the background at church. But the word 'speak' is used 23 times in 1 Corinthians 14, and on every other occasion it refers to publicly addressing the congregation using a spiritual gift, so we cannot change its meaning in the two verses (34-35) which mention women speaking. The word 'speak' does not mean cough, sing, or say 'amen', nor does it forbid women doing any of these things – it refers to publicly addressing the church. Others argue that the women are merely prohibited from 'judging prophecies' (because they might humiliate their husbands). But if so, why does Paul not say this is the reason, and why should unmarried women not be able to ask questions? Paul has long moved on from judging prophecies (v29) and says the reason women can't 'speak' (i.e. publicly address the church) is because it is shameful. Some commentators now argue that these verses were never written by the apostle Paul at all but were added centuries later by a scribe as he copied out Paul's letter. However, there is not one Greek manuscript of this passage that omits these verses, and therefore the evidence overwhelmingly shows they are original. This shows the desperate lengths some will go to avoid what the Bible seems to be saying. Others dismiss Paul as a grumpy old bachelor or male chauvinist. However, these are God's words, not simply Paul's.

The remarkable thing is that many great Brethren Bible teachers have argued for a very different, and at first sight, surprising solution to the apparent contradiction between 1 Corinthians 11:5 and 14:34-35.

I first stumbled on this solution as a young Bible student, working my way through 1 Corinthians for a regular Bible study. I noticed something strange in the Greek text of 1 Corinthians 11: the repeated mention of the Greek word *sunerchomai* (which means 'to come together') in 1 Corinthians 11:17, 18, 20, 33, 34 (and 1 Cor. 14:23, 26). What surprised me was the absence of this same Greek word in the first half of chapter 11. Paul's repeated use of this expression, 'when you come together' in the second half of chapter 11 (along with the expression 'in the church', 1 Cor. 11:18, etc.) emphasizes that the church gatherings are in view in verse 17 onwards, but the absence of these expressions in the first half of 1 Corinthians 11 suggested that Paul is not writing about the church gatherings there. If so, the apparent contradiction between 1 Corinthians 11:5 and 14:34-35 over women speaking in church disappears: it is simply the result of our (false) assumption that the church gatherings are being spoken of in 1 Corinthians 11:2-16.

Initially I thought I was the only person in the world who had noticed this – and kept it to myself. But over the years, I found that many of the best Brethren Bible teachers, ancient and modern, had also seen exactly the same thing and drawn the same conclusion: the evidence for a church setting in 1 Corinthians 11:2-16 is conspicuous by its absence.

- J. N. Darby, writing on 1 Corinthians 11:5, says 'We are not as yet come to the order in the assembly'[71].
- William Macdonald likewise writes, 'Actually meetings of the assembly do not come into view until verse 17 [i.e., the verses about the Lord's Supper], so the instructions in verses 2-16 cannot be confined to church meetings. They apply to whenever a woman prays or prophesies'[72].

- Professor David Gooding similarly argues that the church is not the context or setting in 1 Corinthians 11:2-16. After listing examples of prophets (Elijah, Elisha, Isaiah and Jeremiah) and prophetesses (Anna) whose prophecies were not delivered in the course of formal temple or synagogue services, Gooding writes: 'I imagine then that the early Christians followed the Jewish custom [of women not prophesying or praying audibly in formal worship services]. ... On the point that prophesying took place as much, or more, outside the church as inside – and therefore 1 Corinthians 11:2-16 is not necessarily and primarily concerned only with behaviour in the church – it is perhaps significant that the phrase 'when you come together' is first mentioned at verse 17 and then frequently after that (11:18, 20, 33, 14:23, 26)'[73].

Other Brethren commentators who have argued the same include William Kelly, W. E. Vine, F. B. Hole, W. Hoste, A. Strauch, M. Horlock and J. M. Riddle[74]. Nor is this interpretation limited to Brethren expositors; Lutheran commentators Schlatter, Bachmann and particularly Lenski make powerful arguments[75], and the Presbyterian B. B. Warfield writes about 1 Corinthians 11:5: 'There is nothing said about church in the passage or in the context... There is no reason whatever for believing that "praying and prophesying" in church is meant. Neither was an exercise confined to the church'[76].

This discovery was a great shock to me, because it conflicted with one of the distinctive practices of Brethren assemblies: head covering in church gatherings, something I myself had personally promoted.

Some will object: surely the church gatherings are in view because 1 Corinthians is all about the church, or because Christ's headship is mentioned (1 Cor. 11:3), or 'because of the angels' (1 Cor. 11:10) observing what happens in church. However, 1 Corinthians is about more than church gatherings (e.g. Ch. 7 deals with sexual relations in marriage, Ch. 10 deals with eating meat at an unbeliever's house), Christ is head of more than the church (He is head of 'all principality and power', i.e. angels and demons, Col. 2:10, and will 'head up all things in heaven and earth', Eph. 1:10, see Darby's translation, NET, NLT), while angels watch all we do, not just church life (Dan. 4:13, 17, 23, Zech. 1:7-11, Matt. 18:10). These objections do not prove a church setting.

Head covering is not a major issue among evangelicals generally today. This is because most evangelicals argue that Paul was merely writing about a local custom to do with veils in ancient Corinth, and seeing hats or veils have no moral significance in our society today, we may adopt some culturally-appropriate alternative. However, there are three problems with this view. First, Paul does not argue for head covering in 1 Corinthians 11 based on Corinthian culture, but because of creation. It hardly seems right to say that Paul's reason for his teaching is culture when he himself gives a different reason: creation. Second, evidence strongly suggests that Greek culture did not require women to wear a veil at all. As the *Theological Dictionary of the New Testament* writes, 'It used to be asserted by theologians that Paul was simply endorsing the unwritten law of [Greek] feeling for what was proper. But this view is untenable. To be sure, the veil was not unknown in Greece. ... But it is quite wrong that Greek women were under some kind of compulsion to wear a veil in public ... Passages to the contrary are so numerous and unequivocal that they cannot be offset by two sayings of [Plutarch] ... Hence, veiling was not a general custom'[77]. Third, this 'culturally-relevant' approach to interpreting the Bible allows us to pick and choose which bits of the Bible to obey. By allowing 'culture' to trump God's Word, we open the door to departure from biblical Christianity in any area we choose: doctrine, church life, morality, gender, even homosexuality.

Conservative Brethren, on the other hand, take God's Word here literally, and practice head covering in church meetings. Head covering is a major issue among many Brethren – simply because we want to obey God's Word.

But before I had time to absorb the shock of my discovery that 1 Corinthians 11:2-16 does not mention church gatherings, or consider its implications, I noticed something else surprising in the same chapter.

There are seven references to hair in 1 Corinthians 11. That much is obvious, but was surprised me was that each reference stresses the length of the man's or woman's hair:

- 'that is even all one as if she were shaven' – v5
- 'let her also be shorn' – v6
- 'if it be a shame for a woman to be shorn ...' – v6
- '... or shaven' – v6

- 'if a man have long hair, it is a shame unto him' – v14
- 'if a woman have long hair, it is a glory to her' – v15
- 'for her long hair is given her for a covering' – v15[78].

On each of the seven occasions, the length of the hair is highlighted: men having long hair are shameful, as are women with shorn or shaven heads, while long hair for a woman is her glory. It is not just the end of the passage which talks about the length of the hair – the beginning of the passage does too. By contrast, hats or veils are not mentioned anywhere in the passage.

The main objection to the suggestion this passage is talking about hair lengths is a logical (rather than biblical) argument. It runs like this: if hair were the covering here, this would mean that men must be bald or shave off all their hair. Also, if hair were the covering, then verse 6 would make no sense: it would be saying that if a woman had no hair, let her also be shorn. Seeing that hair as the covering is nonsensical, this cannot be Paul's meaning.

However, this logical *reductio ad absurdum* argument has two logical problems of its own. First, it commits a logical fallacy (the excluded middle) by saying there are only two options in vs4-6: hair or no hair. But this overlooks other options, for when we come down to the end of the passage, where everyone agrees Paul is talking about hair length, there is long hair, and man's-length, short, trimmed, hair. Second, it is guilty of a double-standard, for nobody argues in vs 14-15 for mere hair as the covering. That is, no one says men must be bald in vs14, or that hair (of any length) is a second covering for women (in v15). Instead, *long hair* is the covering which women should have, and men should not.

Did you notice the subtle change, the bait-and-switch, introduced into the argument? The same standard is not being applied consistently to the end of the passage as at the beginning. While hair is rejected as a (ridiculous) option for a covering in vs5-6, when we come down to vs 14-15 it is *long hair* (not mere hair, of any length) that becomes the covering. If, instead, we adopt the same definition of distinctively feminine long hair as the covering throughout, the entire passage makes sense: men should not have long hair like a woman, while women should not cut their hair short to look like a man.

The prominence Paul gives to hair-length rather than hats or veils was, if anything, even more startling than my first discovery. It was not a view of the passage that any Bible teachers I knew had ever advocated.

But, to my surprise, I later found that many Bible scholars have argued for this understanding of the passage. Professor Raymond Collins in his commentary on 1 Corinthians writes, 'Unlike Plutarch, who speaks of the use of the toga (*to himation*) to cover one's head, Paul does not identify any object actually placed on the head. On the other hand, he does talk about cutting and shaving the hair (vv. 5-6) and about the hairdo (vv. 14-15). It is more probable that Paul is talking about hair styles than about wearing a veil or covering one's head with the toga'[79]. Professor Richard Horsley entitles this section of 1 Corinthians, 'Argument concerning Hairstyles'. He writes, 'the passage focuses on hairstyles, not head-covering or veils. Verbs for "having one's hair cut off" and "letting one's hair grow long" appear in vs 6-7 and 14-15 respectively'[80]. One of the most notable scholars advocating this view was Brethren – Professor William J. Martin, head of the department of Semitic Languages at Liverpool University, later Professor of Old Testament at Regent College, Vancouver, who wrote:

> Several indications show beyond reasonable doubt that Paul is using the term "covered" to refer to long hair. First, he uses it in contradistinction to the state of the man who is debarred from "having the hair hanging down" (v. 4). To make the wearing of a head covering the opposite of short hair would be a false antithesis.... [T]here is only one way, one simple, plain, unambiguous, right way to efface the shame of being shorn and that is to have long hair; and that is surely what Paul is saying. Second, nowhere in the passage is any word ever used for a material veil or head-dress. Third, as the forms of the verb *katakalupto* (to cover) found here (vv. 6 and 7) are not construed with an indirect object [i.e. Paul does not say, 'covered *with a veil*'], it is best to take them as passive [i.e. not referring to a veil]. Fourth, in v. 15 Paul states unequivocally that a woman's long hair takes the place of an item of dress[81].

This view is held by many expositors and scholars including Philip Jensen (Dean of St. Andrew's Cathedral, Sydney, ret.), Paul Barnett (Bishop of North Sydney, ret.), David Pawson, Professor Richard Hays, Professor Jerome Murphy-O'Connor, Stephan Lösch, Elizabeth Schüssler Fiorenza, J. B. Hurley and Abel Isaksson[82]. Truth is not determined by counting commentators, but neither is hair styles a fringe view.

Conservative Brethren hold that there is, in effect, a third ordinance of the Christian religion, in addition to baptism and the Lord's Supper: head covering. However, this raises another puzzling contradiction. Why is there no mention of head covering in 1 Timothy 2? This is surprising, because 1 Timothy 2 is dealing with:

a. order in the church (1 Tim. 3:15),
b. prayer in the church (2:1-8),
c. the woman's clothing (2:9-10), and
d. the woman's silence and submission (2:11-15).

1 Timothy 2 would seem to be a most appropriate place for Paul to talk about head covering. We have already noticed one strange omission in 1 Timothy: the Lord's Supper. We suggested this ordinance was so well-known that no special discussion was necessary – like baptism. But there seems no good reason *not* to mention head covering in 1 Timothy 2.

If the head covering were a hat or veil, then 1 Corinthians 11 says that women should have one on whenever they pray (not just in church), while men should never pray without first taking a hat off. But this is hard to accept in practice: would it really be wrong for a man in danger on a motorcycle or building site to pray without first taking off a helmet? Would it be sinful if a mother prayed for a child in danger without first putting on a hat?

But if the passage is instead talking about men and women being distinguished by different hair styles, then all the knotty questions unravel and the puzzles in 1 Corinthians and 1 Timothy are resolved. The head covering is a permanent sign of the difference between the genders, not just one worn at church gatherings, or just during moments of prayer. Nor does 1 Timothy 2 ignore head covering, for the woman's long hair is implied in the warning against 'braided [long] hair' (1 Tim. 2:9).

Now maybe this interpretation of 1 Corinthians 11:2-16 is wrong. But the problem with elevating hat-wearing to an issue of first importance (1 Cor. 15:3), as in many Brethren assemblies – a third Christian ordinance alongside baptism and the Lord's Supper – is that hats are not even mentioned in the passage. As David Pawson writes: 'In the whole passage there is nothing at all about hats – the word doesn't even occur. The word for head covering that Paul uses is 'veil', and this word only occurs once in the whole chapter, in a context that explains how women have been given long hair instead of a veil. So there is not a single sentence that says that women should wear a veil, much less a hat! The section is actually about men's hair being shorter than women's hair'[83].

No ancient Christian creed mentions hat-wearing, nor do any Reformation creeds, or the Anglican Thirty-Nine Articles, or the Westminster Confession. Nor do the early Brethren remark upon it. It is a novel theological fixation, peculiar (almost) to late 20th century Brethren.

Because hat-wearing is an outward rather than inward expression of spirituality, a biblically minor matter that because of its high-visibility takes on a place of major significance, attended by additional rules not stated in Scripture (like at which meetings it must be worn), and often enforced on pain of excommunication, hat-wearing tends to produce a church culture that, contrary to the spirit of Christ, becomes Pharisaical and legalistic.

If brothers or sisters sincerely believe that hat-wearing is what the Bible teaches, then they must follow their conscience and practice it, but to enforce it upon those who are not convinced is foreign to the spirit of the New Testament. Legalism kills, says Paul contending with the Judaizing tendency in 2 Corinthians 3:6, and if hat-wearing is based on the fear of man rather than the freedom of the Spirit of God (2 Cor. 3:17), then all we have is cult-like conformity.

To sum up the matter, hat-wearing is seen by many Christians as odd, based on (flawed) human logic rather than clear statements of Scripture, and contrary to the spirit of Christ with His rejection of mere externalism. By contrast, if this passage is teaching that the covering is the woman's different hair-style, 1 Corinthians 11:2-16 is part of the picture of New Testament simplicity that is also spiritual (rather than legalistic), beautiful and natural (rather than humanly-fabricated), and the Creator's gift (1 Cor. 11:15). The contrast is well summed-up by the poet Cowper: 'Oh how unlike the complex works of man, Heaven's easy, artless, unencumbered plan!'

Finally, this suggestion has two important practical

implications. First, it upholds the authority, sufficiency, and inerrancy of Scripture against claims that 1 Corinthians 11 and 14, or 1 Timothy 2, do not apply to us today, or contradict each other – it is only the false assumption that the church gatherings are in view in 1 Corinthians 11:2-16 that forces a conflict.

Second, it means that our gospel outreach in Brethren assemblies does not need to be hindered or complicated by debates over when hats need to worn. It is difficult enough to get non-Christians to come and hear the gospel without having to first explain what hats or scarves mean. Those who have grown up in hat-wearing churches might be perfectly used to a room full of fancy bonnets, but to any unconverted woman it leads to the instant, off-putting realization that the visitor is the odd one out, the only one not wearing a hat, thus drawing attention to herself. If hat-wearing was pleasing to God, then we should see some good fruit flowing from it. Can anyone point to any blessing that has come from it over the last 70 years? We have closed a thousand assemblies! There are certain issues in the Christian life that are 'hills to die on', but it is hard to think of wearing hats as one of them.

Conclusion

May God give us wisdom, not only to understand His Word aright, but to realize that true spirituality consists, not in an external religion, but in a love for lost souls, and the prioritization of prayer. Here is the source of our power, and where the blessing comes from: prayer.

Chapter Eight

HOW TO CARE FOR THE FLOCK

In his book on assembly decline, Nathan Smith identified leadership as the single greatest issue facing the Brethren. He writes,

> The interviews [with leavers] ... pointed out that the single greatest reason people give for leaving the assemblies is lack of positive leadership, and then the other sources of disaffection flow from this main problem ... A former commended worker from California said in regards to the elders he had worked with: "They will neither lead nor follow nor get out of the way. They feel they have a sacred trust given to them to perpetuate what they think used to be the good old days". Another elder who left and is currently a leader in a parachurch organization said, "There is no procedure for selecting, evaluating and dismissing elders". An elder from Oregon who had left his assembly flatly confirmed, "Weak and insensitive leadership is the main reason people leave the assembly"[84].

Leadership is very important to the health of a church. If a church is not doing very well, it is highly likely it has a leadership problem. Alex Kurian writes:

Lack of positive leadership and pastoral care is another important reason, I believe, as to why people are leaving the assemblies. The word "pastor" has always been an anathema in the assembly circles. Biblical eldership is plural and pastoral. The pastoral aspect of eldership (Acts 20:28; 1 Pet.5:2) is not emphasized in our teaching. Most of our books and commentaries also are silent about it. Whenever we refer to the word "Pastor", our single aim has been to prove that the denominational pastoral system is wrong. We always portray the word in a negative way. I have never heard in my life a positive biblical teaching on the aspect of pastoral leadership in the assembly circles. Thank God, that situation is slowly changing, at least with some concerned Bible teachers. There is no "pastor" over a church, but there are "pastors" (shepherds) in a church. Our whole emphasis has been on plurality of leadership and unknowingly, we have neglected the pastoral aspect of church leadership. This may be an over-reaction to the denominational system of one-man leadership/pastor ruling the assembly. Let us be careful not to throw the baby out with the bath water. We need more spiritual leaders in our assemblies with caring and shepherding hearts, who are sensitive to the struggles and problems of believers[85].

Leadership is a word some Christians dislike. I have some sympathy with people who have an allergic reaction to the word leadership, because our Lord Jesus said much more about serving than leading. However, both the word and the concept of leadership are found throughout the Bible.

Later in this chapter we will look at what 1 Timothy 3 says about leadership in the church. Verse 1 teaches that a desire for leadership in the church is not sinful: 'if anyone desires the position of an overseer, he desires a good work'. In fact, spiritual leadership is essential.

Why are spiritual leaders essential? Because, as we saw in 1 Timothy 1, good teaching is vital for the health of the church. Who is going to stand up for healthy teaching in the church? Who is going to be brave enough to say that some things that are being taught are false-teaching or just empty words that waste our time? Spiritual leaders – that's who. 1 Timothy chapters 1 and 2 talk about the priority of prayer for the sake of the gospel. If a church is going to see real prayer happening, it will need leaders to promote it. If effective gospel outreach is going to happen, again, it will need leaders. Who is going to stand up and say that God has different roles for men and women in the church, as we saw in 1 Timothy 2?

We need leaders who will stand for what the Word of God says and take the church forward in God's ways. The church will drift if it has leaders who are like reeds blown by the wind. Spiritual leadership is necessary if God's work is to be protected from spiritual dangers, and the church is going to grow. But we also need leaders like Nehemiah who truly love God's people and care for the flock. The church will not do well if it has power-hungry people ambitious for position.

Biblical Leadership

Before we look at some reasons Brethren assemblies have

struggled over the issue of leadership, we must first point out some positives about leadership in Brethren assemblies. In particular, there are four biblical truths about church leadership Brethren have followed.

Church Leadership in New Testament was Plural, rather than a 'one-man show'. Notice the following verses which show multiple elders in every church:

- the Church in Jerusalem was governed by elders. See Acts 11:30, 15: 2, 4, 16:4 and 21:18.
- In Acts 14:23, Paul and Barnabus 'appointed elders in every church'.
- In Acts 20:17, Paul called for the elders of the Church in Ephesus to meet him in Miletus.
- Paul directs Titus to 'appoint elders in every city' (Titus 1:5).
- James writes: 'Is anyone sick among you? Let him call for the elders of the Church'.
- In Philippians 1:1, Paul addresses his letter 'to all the saints in Christ Jesus who are in Philippi, with the overseers and deacons'.

John Stott writes:

> What model of the church, then, should we keep in our minds? The traditional model is that of the pyramid, with the pastor perched precariously on its pinnacle, like a little pope in his own church, while the laity are arrayed beneath him in serried ranks of inferiority. It is a totally unbiblical image, because the

New Testament envisages not a single pastor with a docile flock but both a plural oversight and an every-member ministry'[86].

Stephen Short points out that in Paul's opening greeting to the Philippians, there is:

> no mention of the church's 'minister', where such mention, surely, would have been expected. Indeed, in the introduction of none of the New Testament Epistles is the 'minister' addressed; nor, at the conclusion of any of the New Testament Epistles are greetings sent to him – even (as in the epistles to the Romans and the Colossians) where greetings are sent to many people. One might even go so far as to submit that in no New Testament letter to a local Christian church is there any allusion made anywhere to what the author might have termed the 'minister' of that church, or the 'pastor' of that church; and it is difficult to suggest any other reason for this than that 'ministers' and 'pastors' as we know them today did not then exist. What did then exist, and what fulfilled the function which is fulfilled now by 'ministers' and 'pastors', was a body of 'elders', or 'overseers', or 'bishops', so that Paul could here write: 'Paul and Timotheus, the servants of Jesus Christ, to all the saints in Christ Jesus which are at Philippi, with the bishops'[87].

If you will pardon me for putting it this way, in the New Testament, there was no Reverend Rufus, or Bishop

Blastus, or Pastor Persis. There is only one exception to this rule in the New Testament, an exception that proves the rule: Diotrophes who wanted to have the pre-eminence (3 John 9), and acted like the boss of the church, but was condemned for it.

Secondly, Elders, Overseers and Shepherds are Synonymous Terms, not different offices. In the New Testament, elders were exactly the same people as shepherds (i.e. pastors) and overseers (i.e. bishops), meaning that there were no separate offices above or alongside elders. We see that elders, overseers and shepherds were different terms for the same people in the following verses:

- In Acts 20, Paul called for the *elders* of the Church in Ephesus (v17). Then in verse 28, Paul says to them: 'Therefore take heed to yourselves and to all the flock, among which the Holy Spirit has made you *overseers*, to *shepherd* the Church of God which He purchased with His own blood'.
- In 1 Peter 5, Peter uses all three of these same expressions again when writing to the *elders* (v1), urging them to *shepherd* the flock of God (v2), serving as *overseers* (v2).
- In Titus 1, Paul tells Titus to appoint *elders* (1:5). In verse 7, listing their qualifications, he then says, 'For an *overseer* must be blameless ...'.
- In 1 Timothy 3:1-7 we read about the qualifications of *overseers*. However, the qualifications of *elders* in

Titus 1 are virtually identical, suggesting they are the same office.

Thus, these three terms elder, overseer and shepherd appear to be applied interchangeably to the same leaders, and merely describe different aspects of their roles as leaders. 'Elders' describes their maturity, 'overseers' their authority and 'shepherds' their activity.

Alexander Strauch says: 'The New Testament does not give the slightest hint that the eldership is to be presided over by a pastor. There is no office of pastor, only the offices of elder and deacon'[88] (by 'pastor' here, Strauch means the Western concept of a single, separate, leader of a church, distinct from the elders).

Nor were overseers (i.e. bishops) a higher level of church government over elders, as Episcopalians (e.g. Anglicans[89]) hold. The New Testament evidence shows that elders and overseers were exactly the same men.

How Church Elders were Appointed. The New Testament says seven things about appointing elders:

- Elders were Appointed by the apostles and others (Acts 14:23, Titus 1:5).
- Elders are Made by God (Acts 20:28 – 'the Holy Spirit has made you overseers')
- Elders are Gifted (Ephesians 4:11 – pastor/shepherd is a spiritual gift)
- Eldership is an Aspiration (1 Tim. 3:1 – 'if any man desires eldership')

- Eldership is a Work, not simply an office, which implies he should already be doing it (1 Tim. 3:1 – 'if any desires eldership, he desires a good work')
- There are Qualifications (1 Tim. 3:1-7, Titus 1)
- Elders are Recognized (1 Thess. 5:12 – someone can only lead with the consent of those being led).

The appointment of elders in Brethren assemblies has been an area of confusion. However, the Bible gives clear guidelines for what sort of person should be considered for eldership, and how they should be appointed.

Another problem that has hampered Brethren assemblies historically is the idea, taught originally by Darby, that there are no elders today. Because elders in the New Testament were appointed by apostles (or 'apostolic delegates', e.g. Titus), and we have no apostles, so we cannot have elders. However, this objection invents the office of 'apostolic delegate' out of thin air – it is not a biblical term. The fact that Paul gave Timothy and Titus a list of qualifications for prospective elders suggests that they did not possess any special powers of mystical intuition to appoint elders, and further means that these lists of qualifications have been given by God for our ongoing need to appoint elders. John Riddle writes: 'The idea that we cannot have elders today is sheer nonsense. We have the word of God to lead us and teach us'[90].

What Leaders Do. One of the words for church leaders is a shepherd or pastor, and this word teaches us about the work of a church leader. To understand what a shepherd does, the best place to turn is Psalm 23. Here are four things a shepherd does:

1. Shepherds Feed. This is a shepherd's primary task – to feed the flock. 'The Lord is my Shepherd, I shall not want. He makes me to lie down in green pastures, He leads me beside the still waters'.
2. Shepherds Lead. 'He leads me beside the still waters, He restores my soul, He leads me in the paths of righteousness for His name's sake'. For a shepherd to be a leader, he must have vision, foresight, and awareness of pressing needs and possible solutions. The shepherd does not force the sheep to go before him along the path. Rather, the sheep follow because they trust the wisdom, courage and care of the shepherd.
3. Shepherds Guard. 'Yea, though I walk through the valley of the shadow of death, I will fear no evil for You are with me ... You prepare a table before me in the presence of my enemies'.
4. Shepherds Care. 'Yea, though I walk through the valley of the shadow of death, I will fear no evil, for You are with me, Your rod and staff, they comfort me'. A shepherd must have a real love for the people of God. Otherwise, he will not bother to see that they are fed, led and protected.

1 Timothy 3: Leadership in the Church

What does spiritual leadership involve? 1 Timothy 3 says that the church needs godly leaders. I suggest we learn four things about leadership in this chapter.

Leadership is about Character

Most of the requirements for leadership in this chapter have to do with the character of the leader. Verse 2 says, 'the overseer must be blameless (that is, not perfect, but untainted by scandal), the husband of one wife, temperate (lit. sober), sound-minded, of good behaviour (or respectable)'. Verse 3 says, 'not given to wine, not violent, not quarrelsome, not covetous (lit. a lover of money)'. Verse 7 says, 'Moreover he must have a good testimony among those who are outside, lest he fall into reproach and the snare of the devil'.

Someone has defined leadership as influence, and the most important way we can influence others is by our character and godly lifestyle. Dwight Eisenhower, the World War Two General, and later US President said:

> In order to be a leader, a man must have followers. And to have followers, a man must have their confidence. Hence the supreme quality for a leader is unquestionable integrity. Without it, no real success is possible, no matter whether it is on … a football field, in an army, or in an office. If a man's associates find him guilty of phoniness, if they find that he lacks forthright integrity, he will fail. His teachings and actions must square with each other. The first great need, therefore, is integrity and high purpose.

Just the same, in church leadership, the most important thing is character. How do we develop godly character? By spending time with the Lord, sitting at His feet to hear His Word, being built up in our own faith, so that we are full of joy and peace and love, and can help others.

Leadership is about Caring
The second thing that stands out in 1 Timothy 3 is that leadership involves caring. Verses 4 & 5 say, 'one who rules his own house well, having his children in submission with all reverence, (for if a man does not know how to rule his own house, how will he take care of the church of God?)'. The parallel is drawn here between a man's family life and his church life. Just as he loves and cares for his family, so too he should care for the church. In verse 15 the church is called the house of God. The church is a house – it should be a place where God's family are cared for.

This is why the word 'shepherd' is used for church leaders in various places – shepherds care for sheep. Peter writes to the elders in 1 Peter 5:1-4 and says, 'Shepherd the flock of God which is among you, serving as overseers'. Paul, speaking to the elders of the church in Ephesus in Acts 20 says, 'take heed to yourselves and to all the flock, among which the Holy Spirit has made you overseers, to shepherd the church of God'. Christian leaders not only need to have godly character, but they also need to care for God's people like shepherds.

What does caring for God's people look like in practical terms? Pastoral care (i.e. shepherd care) involves getting alongside people and getting to know them (that's why hospitality is listed as a characteristic of an overseer in the church). Pastoral care involves giving practical help in people's problems, and praying with them.

But the most important thing about shepherd care is

this: sharing God's Word with people. Do you remember what the Lord Jesus said to Peter in John 21:15-17? 'Feed my sheep, feed my lambs'. The greatest need sheep have is to be fed. This is why another one of the characteristics of an elder in verse 3 is that he is 'able to teach'. An elder is not someone who just gives out a song at the breaking of bread, or prays at the beginning of a meeting. An elder is someone who feeds the flock from God's Word.

Titus 1:9-11 says that the elder must be a man who is 'holding fast the faithful word as he has been taught, that he may be able, by sound doctrine, both to exhort and convict those who contradict. [10] For there are many insubordinate, both idle talkers and deceivers, especially those of the circumcision, [11] whose mouths must be stopped' ....

An elder must be able to publicly defend the truth against false-teachers and also to encourage God's people by healthy teaching. That doesn't mean they have to preach like C. H. Spurgeon or Billy Graham. But they need to know God's Word, and be able to teach God's Word, privately and also in the church.

One of the best ways of doing this sort of pastoral care is by meeting up with another person once a week to read God's Word and pray together. It does not need to take too much time. It just involves getting alongside others in God's Word and prayer, and encouraging them in their Christian walk.

The Lord Jesus Christ is the best illustration of caring shepherd leadership. Isaiah 40:11 says, 'He will feed His flock like a shepherd; He will gather the lambs with His arm, and carry them in His bosom, and gently lead those who are with young'.

Sadly, some Christian leaders, instead of being like a shepherd, are more like a sheepdog, snapping and biting at the sheep, driving them away. These elders think they can rule over the flock like a lord, and treat them harshly like a dictator – but this scatters the flock. So, here is the second thing about good leadership: it involves shepherd care of God's people.

Leadership is about Courage

The third thing we learn about leadership is that it involves courage – the courage to lead.

As Christians, we have been given the task of bringing the gospel to others around us who are perishing and helping support them once they're saved. For us to do this, we need leaders who have courage and wisdom to lead. Three times in 1 Timothy 3 we read about overseers being those who 'rule' (but a better translation is 'lead'): one who leads his own house well (v4), and then similarly in v5 – 'he who leads his own house well', and then we read about the deacon over in v12, 'ruling (or leading) their children and their own houses well'. Paul's argument is, if you can't lead your own house, how can you be a leader in the church of God?

Leadership involves being bold, taking risks, and taking on challenges. Leadership is about faith, stepping out in obedience to what God calls us to do, and finding that, even though we seem to be stepping out into an uncertain future, the Lord is with us.

Winston Churchill is considered one of history's greatest leaders, becoming Prime Minister of Great Britain at the darkest point of World War Two, and leading it to victory over Adolf Hitler. What were his characteristics as a leader? He was marked by great courage, vision, communication, and passion. He said,

> You ask, what is our policy? I will say: It is to wage war, by sea, land and air, with all our might and with all the strength that God can give us: to wage war against a monstrous tyranny, never surpassed in the dark, lamentable catalogue of human crime. That is our policy. You ask, what is our aim? I can answer in one word: It is victory, victory at all costs, victory in spite of all terror, victory, however long and hard the road may be; for without victory, there is no survival.

On another occasion, he said, "Never give in - never, never, never, never, in nothing great or small, large or petty, never give in except to convictions of honour and good sense."

Not only do we need leaders to help the church reach out in evangelism, but we also need leaders to face the complex challenges we have in the church. Someone else has said that leadership is problem solving – facing up to the challenges honestly (not hiding from them – sticking our heads in the stand). Leadership requires wisdom to solve these problems, and remember: the Word of God speaks about two sorts of wisdom – there is worldly wisdom (which James calls earthly, sensual, and devilish) and then there is the wisdom from above.

We need wise leaders. Leaders gather knowledge: leaders are readers. Leaders seek good, godly advice. Leadership involves having a plan. Think of the great leaders of the Bible and human history. Godly leaders are like the men we read about in 1 Chronicles 12:32, 'the sons of Issachar who had understanding of the times, to know what Israel ought to do'.

Where do we get that sort of wisdom and courage from? From God, by His Spirit – the Spirit of wisdom and knowledge, the one who strengthens us with power in the inner man. Think of all the great leaders of the Old Testament – God's Spirit came up them. Leaders need to be filled with God's Spirit.

Bill Newman gives a great definition of a leader in his book, *The Ten Laws of Leadership*: A leader is someone who knows the way, goes the way and shows the way. That is, a leader knows the way, having wisdom and spiritual understanding, a leader goes the way, having courage, boldness, and faith, and a leader shows the way, by their character, example and teaching.

Leadership is Christ-Focused

Lastly, I suggest that godly church leadership is Christ-focused. Verses 14-16 tell us that the church is the house of God, the church of the living God, the pillar and ground of the truth. And what truth does this pillar, the Church, exist to uphold? Verse 16 tells us: the truth is all about our Lord Jesus Christ.

- He is God manifested in the flesh – a declaration of His deity and humanity.

- He was justified in the Spirit – justified, as in vindicated, by His resurrection, for after He was condemned to death by men, God glorified Him
- He was seen by angels – the One angels dared not look upon in heaven
- He was preached among the Gentiles – His message is being preached to all people, even the far off Gentiles.
- He was believed on in the world – despite being rejected by His own nation, yet people are believing in Christ, and being saved by simple faith.
- He was received up in glory – rejected on earth, He was given Heaven's highest place of honour.

What is all this saying? That Christ Himself must be at the centre of Church life and therefore church leadership must love Christ and keep the focus on His person and work.

Problems in Leadership in Brethren Assemblies

Brethren assemblies have the outward form of biblical leadership, but we have many problems in practice. In my nearly 30 years of experience in full-time work in fellowship with Brethren assemblies, I have noticed ten different types of difficulties with leadership in Brethren assemblies:

1. There has been a lack of teaching about the biblical role of elders, their qualifications, their appointment, and their duties. For example, there is confusion about how elders are appointed. To quote the words of one believer, 'After 39 years in the assembly, I have

no idea how elders are chosen'[91]. This leads on to a second problem,

2. The appointment of unsuitable elders. Because there is not enough teaching about the qualifications and duties of elders, elders have been appointed who were not suited to the job. I know of one assembly where the 'leading brother' passed away one week, and on the next Sunday one of the elders stood up and announced that anyone who wished to become an elder should come and speak to him. The result was the appointment of people who were not qualified. One of Nathan Smith's interviewees gives another example, 'Our assembly came out of a tight assembly background and we retained some of the exclusive tendencies, such as the nonrecognition of elders. This created real problems because when we began to recognize elders, there were men who had been there for 50 years. They just assumed leadership roles and there was no way to get these men out'[92]. Some think they should be elders simply because of their age, or the length of time they have been in the assembly, or because of their standing in the business world.

3. Lack of good Bible teaching by elders. Paul reminded the Ephesian elders of his three-year ministry among them teaching the Word of God, in effect urging them to continue doing the same: 'I commend you to God and to the word of His grace, which is able to build you up' (Acts 20:32). But many Brethren elders have neither gift nor interest in teaching God's Word. In the New Testament, an elder is not just someone

who can give out a hymn or pray, or open the doors on time, or book visiting speakers; an elder must be someone who can handle God's Word well. Why? Because a shepherd's primary job is to feed sheep. Some would argue that an elder need not be a public teacher, but simply be able to teach privately, however there are several problems with this argument. No one in the secular world would call a person a teacher if they were unable to stand in front of a class and teach publicly. The requirements for elders in Titus 1 clearly state that an overseer be able to publicly refute false teaching as well as provide sound teaching that encourages God's people. The same expression 'able to teach' in the qualifications of an elder in 1 Tim. 3:2 is also used to describe the 'servant of the Lord' in 2 Timothy 2:24, and being a servant of the Lord (like Timothy) would involve public (as well as private) teaching. Further, in Ephesians 4:11, we read, 'He (Christ) gave some to be apostles, some prophets, some evangelists, and some pastors and teachers', and whereas the first four gifts have the word 'some' attached to them, the last word 'teachers' does not. The effect of this, Greek scholars suggest, is to link the last two gifts as almost synonymous terms; in other words, shepherd-teachers. In any case, the argument that a man could teach privately might be okay if someone was actually engaged in doing it, but usually, men who do not teach publicly are not busy doing it privately either. The result of the lack of good teaching by elders is that the flock is not fed.

4. Eldership seen as a position of power. Instead of being spiritual shepherds, elders are a board of directors making executive decisions. But while the elders do have to make decisions on some matters, their main work is to shepherd the flock by feeding, caring for, leading and guarding it. The argument ('a person does not have to be able to teach publicly') is sometimes used to justify people being appointed as elders for largely political reasons (e.g. there are a lack of elders and someone else is needed). Some are appointed as elders because they are 'yes-men', while others far more qualified are excluded because they might 'rock the boat'. Many younger people growing up in assemblies think of the elders as the board who make all the decisions, a political office rather than a spiritual work. This is because they must get all their suggestions approved by the elders. But this neglects the spiritual side of the elder's work.

5. Lack of pastoral care. Because the 'open meeting' requires Christians to be spiritual self-starters, able to feed themselves and contribute to the meeting out of their own personal walk with the Lord, elders have tended not to engage in much pastoral work. In many assemblies, the only time members get a visit from the elders is when there is a problem, either spiritually or with health. In many assemblies, Sunday 'meetings' are the 'be-all and end-all', but there is much to be gained by visiting the flock and encouraging them in spiritual growth. Hospitality is another good way to show pastoral care. Elders also need to invest time in

meeting up with younger Christians to read God's Word together and pray. Alex Kurian writes, 'In assemblies where there is more responsible pastoral care, we see growth and blessing. Meaningful pastoral care is the strength of many evangelical churches. Pentecostal and Charismatic churches all over the world attract more people to their fold, not through their doctrine, but by gracious and caring pastoral ministry. It is a general complaint or accusation against us that assemblies are not ideal places for hurting people and people who go through various problems of life. Many people who go through trying situations of life usually leave the assemblies knowing that they will not "survive" there as there is no ministry towards them (especially those who are in the midst of marriage/family crisis). Even the young generation among the Brethren constantly accuse us as non-compassionate, judgmental, ungracious, and ministering only to "perfect" people, and holding on to the "truth" without "grace." Have we been too harsh and ungracious in applying the Scripture, clinging on to the letter of the law than the spirit of it? I believe, all these problems have something to do with the lack of caring, and trained pastoral leadership. Many assemblies are led by people who may be faithful, but lack leadership skills. We all know that this is true though many do not want to admit it'[93].

6. Lack of teaching about the biblical role of deacons. Many assemblies have elders but have neglected to

appoint deacons. For some smaller assemblies, deacons may not be necessary, but for larger assemblies, deacons can relieve the elders of practical tasks so that the elders can focus on the spiritual needs of pastoral care of the flock.

7. Elders doing deacon work. Due to a lack of teaching about the differences between elder and deacon work, in many assemblies elders are in fact functioning simply as deacons. They are involved in building maintenance, looking after the finances, administration, and correspondence – all tasks which properly belong to the office of deacons.

8. Lack of leadership and vision. Many elders are busy attending to the immediate needs of the assembly. Their mind is continually occupied with the present needs, and the result is short-term thinking rather than a vision for the future. Elders should be appointing deacons to look after some of the immediate tasks and delegating jobs to others. The word for these immediate needs is 'management', not 'leadership'. True spiritual leadership involves 'motivating, mobilizing, resourcing and directing people to pursue a jointly shared vision from God'[94].

9. Lack of leadership training and development. Elders need to be looking to the future by training up godly men to be the next generation of elders. They need to be encouraging young men and investing in the future by giving them opportunity to grow through serving. They need to be teaching them about the role, duties, qualifications and appointment of elders.

10. Lack of full-time elders. Finally, in some large assemblies, the elders need to consider appointing full-time elders or reimbursing some current elders for sacrificing some of their time to serve the Lord (1 Tim. 5:17-18). As verse 18 shows, Paul is saying here that some elders should be financially recompensed for the time they take in teaching and shepherding the flock. Alex Kurian writes, 'Another major issue facing the assemblies is the lack of full-time elders. We have never encouraged this idea. I have even heard some of our teachers speaking against this idea. This is never a prayer item in the assembly prayer meetings. We do not even recognize the need for it! It is true that many of our elders along with their secular employment try to do their best with great sacrifice on their part. But we have to be more practical and realistic. In the fast-paced busy world in which we live, along with the various challenges facing us every day both at work and at home, there are lots of factors that can make things harder. An elder's responsibilities at work, home, and church create a real time crunch. Hence, many of them are not able to do their pastoral work as of high priority, though they may have a heart to do it. This is a built-in weakness which we have ignored. This is an undeniable fact and no theology can eliminate it. This practical problem has nothing to do with the elder's sincerity, commitment or honesty; it is simply the reality of life. I believe it is high time for assemblies to think more seriously, encouraging some of our

elders to be full-time shepherds for the flock of God. I wish if we could make this a matter of urgent concern and prayer and seek the Lord's will in this matter. We have to have practical and remedial measures to bridge the gap in pastoral ministries in the assemblies. Implementing the principles in 1 Tim. 5:17-18 can be of much help to us in this crisis'[95].

Conclusion

When we look at biblical leadership, the standards are so high, the responsibility can seem overwhelming. It is difficult getting the balance between caring and being courageous – we can be too soft and not stand up for the truth, or we can be too strong and domineering.

God isn't calling for perfection from us. That's one of the reasons the Bible teaches plural leadership in the church, not a 'one-man band'. Scripture teaches a leadership team where men with different strengths can help each other and complement one another. Some might be better teachers, others better at evangelism, others at pastoral care, and others at administration.

God is calling for leaders. In fact, God is calling for all of us, whether leaders or not, to be people of character, people who care for others, people of courage to step out for God, and people who are Christ-focused. That, after all, is how anyone becomes a leader.

Chapter Nine

THE SUPREME VIRTUE

As I mentioned in the first chapter, when I arrived in London in 1993, I felt that God was wanting me to visit Brook Street Chapel in Tottenham, and I eventually stayed there for a year. But I also visited several other assemblies. One of the reasons I stayed at Brook Street, as opposed to other assemblies, was because of the friendly welcome I received and the hospitality I was shown. Other assemblies seemed to be slightly frosty and aloof. But at Tottenham, I felt the warmth of Christian love.

In the last two chapters of 1 Timothy, Paul writes about another important aspect of church life: the need for love and care. In 1 Timothy 5:1-2 he says:

> Do not rebuke an older man, but exhort him as a father, younger men as brothers, ² older women as mothers, younger as sisters, with all purity.

The church is to be like a family – with older men respected as fathers, older women as mothers, and younger men and women treated as brothers and sisters. This is because the church is the 'house of God' (1 Tim. 3:15), God's family.

In 1 Timothy 5:3-16, Paul writes about the care of

widows: 'Honor widows who are really widows' (verse 3). The word 'honour' here has a double meaning and here teaches 'help financially'. Paul goes on to speak about the financial support of elders who are sacrificing time to teach and shepherd the flock (1 Tim. 5:17-25). Then, at the beginning of chapter 6, he teaches that slaves should honour masters, particularly believing ones (1 Tim. 6:1-2): 'because they are brethren ... believers and beloved'. They were all part of the one family.

This brings us back to our Lord Jesus' words:

> A new commandment I give to you, that you love one another; as I have loved you, that you also love one another. ³⁵ By this all will know that you are My disciples, if you have love for one another (John 13:34-35).

We see the importance of this principle of love in action in the early chapters of Acts among the first Christians. Love for one another, fellowship together, and practical care for the needy, were notable features of the early Church:

- And they continued steadfastly in the apostles' doctrine and fellowship, in the breaking of bread, and in prayers. (Acts 2:42)
- Now all who believed were together, and had all things in common, ⁴⁵ and sold their possessions and goods, and divided them among all, as anyone had need. ⁴⁶ So continuing daily with one accord in the temple, and breaking bread from house to house, they ate their

- food with gladness and simplicity of heart, (Acts 2:44-46)
- Now the multitude of those who believed were of one heart and one soul; neither did anyone say that any of the things he possessed was his own, but they had all things in common. [33] And with great power the apostles gave witness to the resurrection of the Lord Jesus. And great grace was upon them all. [34] Nor was there anyone among them who lacked; for all who were possessors of lands or houses sold them, and brought the proceeds of the things that were sold, [35] and laid them at the apostles' feet; and they distributed to each as anyone had need. (Acts 4:32-35).

Love is supremely important. In a day of celebrity preachers, we only have to read 1 Corinthians 13 to see that love is superior to any spiritual gift. Paul said:

> though I have the gift of prophecy, and understand all mysteries and all knowledge, and though I have all faith, so that I could remove mountains, but have not love, I am nothing. (1 Cor. 13:2)

This brings us back to the first principle of the early Brethren: love for all those who are Christ's. Sadly, the history of the Brethren since has often been marked by the very opposite. A lack of true Christian love has been a major reason why many people have left. Instead of love for Christ and love for His people, a petty legalism, tyrannical and bitter, has sometimes been given the first place in Brethren ecclesiology.

The Lesson of the Exclusive Brethren

To see why love is such an important principle, it is worth looking 'over the fence' at the Exclusive Brethren and thinking about what has happened to them.

In addition to John Nelson Darby's original teaching on the unity of all true believers, he also developed strong views in a very different direction: the necessity of separation from evil. One particular doctrine that dominated Darby's thought was his theory of 'the Church in ruins'. Just as we see human failure in every age throughout the Bible (e.g. before the flood or in the history of Israel), so Darby held that the Church age was also a failure. Darby even held that the apostles were guilty of 'moral departure from God' by staying in Jerusalem too long and failing to preach the gospel to all the world. Darby's policy therefore was to urge believers to separate from corrupt churches. He wrote, 'God's unity is always founded on separation, since sin came into the world. "Get thee out" is the first word of God's call'.

Exclusivism – the principle of separation from evil – has a twin brother: division. Instead of love for God's people, divisions and in-fighting became the trademark of the Exclusive Brethren.

In 1848, Darby accused B. W. Newton of false-teaching on a point of doctrine. Darby excommunicated not only Newton but the church in Plymouth which had 'tolerated' Newton's teaching. Darby then proceeded to excommunicate Bethesda church in Bristol for having received individual believers from Newton's church, on the grounds that the Bristol brethren had not investigated the matter and were thus 'morally identified with the evil' (even though the brethren at Bristol had interviewed the believers and satisfied themselves that they did not hold the heretical views).

Following this, Darby embarked on a program of relentless propaganda against the church in Bristol, as a result of which many other churches were bullied into condemning it too. E. H. Broadbent wrote:

> By dint of constant repetition this circle of churches came to believe, in all sincerity, that Bethesda had been cut off for holding Newton's error, an error which he himself had repudiated, and which the church at Bethesda had never entertained. So consistently was this system carried out that Negro brethren in the West Indies had to judge the Bethesda question, and Swiss peasants in their Alpine villages were obliged to examine the errors attributed to Newton and condemn them (*The Pilgrim Church*).

The result of this 'purge' was that Darby had created a circle of fellowship of 'pure' churches which excluded all others. For some years, all went well. But then, in 1876, Dr. Cronin, one of the founding members of the Brethren movement, visited a fellowship of Christians on the Isle of Wight that had left the Church of England and had decided to become a Brethren congregation. An Exclusive Brethren congregation already existed in the same town, albeit riddled with strife and argument (Darby himself called it 'rotten'). Dr. Cronin, upon returning to his home fellowship in Kennington, was assailed for his attack on 'the ground of the one body' – which, simply translated, means visiting a fellowship not within the 'club network'.

H. A. Ironside, himself a member of the Grant Exclusives, in a chapter titled 'Playing Church', diagnoses the problem as 'the growing ecclesiastical pretension, spiritual pride, and scarcely-concealed contempt on the part of many for less-instructed believers'[96]. After some months of dispute in Kennington, Ironside writes, 'the patriarchal offender was excommunicated and for months set back with the tears streaming down his face as his brethren remembered the Lord, and he, the first of them all was in the place of the immoral man or the blasphemer. Finally he promised that, although unable to confess his act as sin, he would not offend in the same way again out of deference to the consciences of his brethren but was still kept under the ban. Is it any wonder that some critic said of the Brethren that they are "people who are very particular about breaking bread, but very careless about breaking hearts"?'[97]. 'While the matter was still up for discussion at Kennington, other assemblies were greatly roused and were trying to hurry them to definite action. At Ramsgate a majority party, led by a fiery zealot, Mr. Jull, proceeded to excommunicate the entire Kennington Meeting for its dilatoriness in dealing with the "wicked old doctor"'[98].

One division followed another. A minority of the Ramsgate meeting refused to go along with the excommunication of the Kennington meeting and walked out to start their own meeting. In due course, they were excommunicated by the main Park Street meeting in

London who declared that they were 'off the ground of the church of God'. This decision, taken by the 'High Church party' among the Exclusives, was not followed by some of the more moderate members of the Exclusives, including the influential William Kelly, hence the start of the Kelly branch of the Exclusives. The aging Darby himself was deeply saddened by these events, but unable to stop the relentless in-fighting that his twisted vision of the church had set in train.

Similarly, in 1883, there was a division in Canada between what came to be known as the Grant exclusives and the rest, over the question of whether a person is sealed by the Holy Spirit (a) when he believes the gospel, or (b) when he trusts in Christ. There were other divisions among the Exclusives: in 1885 (the Stuart division, over the difference between a believer's 'standing' and 'condition'), 1890 (the Bexhill division) and the Glanton division in 1908.

We see a pattern here: if the principle of Christian unity is 'separation from evil', the result is endless division. W. H. Griffith-Thomas, the Anglican theologian (who was in substantial agreement with the Brethren on prophetic matters) said: 'The Brethren are remarkable people for rightly dividing the Word of truth and wrongly dividing themselves'.

James Taylor Snr., before becoming the undisputed leader (he led the Exclusives from 1910-53), had caused some disquiet among English brethren by teaching that salvation was only to be found in the assembly.

Michael Bachelard describes the way Taylor gradually

increased his power and control over the Exclusives: 'Taylor also began introducing the notion, further developed by his son, JT Junior, that when a spiritual man said something in an assembly, the Holy Spirit was present. This meant that the words of the Exclusive Brethren leaders provided continuing revelation, or 'new light', which was equivalent to biblical scripture. One of Taylor's addresses was entitled, 'The Assembly: Its Heavenly Character' and, shortly before his death in 1953, he declared: 'The greatest thing I know of at the present time on earth is the presence of the Holy Spirit in the assembly'. This doctrine greatly freed the church's leaders from the close biblical readings and the heavy, convoluted intellectualism of Darby, and allowed them to lay down edicts in the name of one branch of the Holy Trinity, the Spirit. The new, post-Glanton administrative mechanism could then enforce these interpretations as law around the Exclusive Brethren world'[99].

James Taylor Snr also introduced the idea of an 'unbroken line' of spiritual leaders – the 'Elect Vessels': Darby, Raven and Taylor. It was the Exclusive version of the Roman Catholic doctrines of Apostolic Succession and Papal Infallibility, a comparison that would have horrified Darby. The way was paved for the Exclusives to become a full-blown cult.

The Brethren historian Dronsfield describes the six year struggle over who would replace Jim Taylor Snr.: the leadership was fought for with a 'rivalry ... which resembled the struggle for power in the Kremlin after the death of Stalin'[100].

Eventually James Taylor Junior (who ruled from 1959 to 1970) became the undisputed leader. His main challenger Gerald R. Cowell lost the confidence of his brethren and was excommunicated for suggesting that great numbers had left the Exclusives (under James Taylor Snr) as a result of the Galatian heresy (i.e. legalism). In other words, Cowell was too soft.

The high tide of legalism came in the reign of Jim Taylor Jnr, who issued 390 directives during his time at the top from 1959-1970. Rules that Exclusive Brethren had to abide by included no smoking, no gambling, (although drinking was fine), no radio, no TV, no fax machines, no automatic garage door openers (these rely on radio waves, which are evil), no internet (for a long time, it was no computers at all, and mobile phones are now allowed, apparently, though once banned), no university education, no voting, no eating with non-members, no eating at restaurants, no staying at hotels or motels, no apartments (because of shared walls or drainpipes), no cinema or theatre, no novels, no CDs, no pets and no holidays (except staying with other sect members).

Under James Taylor Jnr, the Exclusives took the doctrine of separation to heights never scaled before. Exclusives were forbidden from having any social contact with outsiders, whether ungodly or Christian. On the basis of 1 Cor. 5:11, Exclusives were banned from eating or drinking even with family members who were not part of the sect. The result was tragic for many. Stories abound of families ripped apart because of one spouse who was not converted (or even if a member of the sect broke one of the rules), from whom the rest of the family was separated. Spouses who were 'withdrawn from' would be divorced at the instigation of the sect and the children would be barred from ever seeing this parent again, lest they too should be drawn away 'into the world'. While the husband was away at work, wives and children would be taken away from the family home, never to be contacted again. Many lives and families were destroyed.

Ron Fawkes, a former Australian leader of the sect describes the result: 'I was 17 in 1960, and I remember the pain and anguish, the awful situation of spouses who were married for 40-odd years forced to separate from their unbelieving husbands, who had before coexisted quite happily and normally'[101]. Even members caught speaking to loved ones who were 'out' were subject to assembly discipline. Fawkes did not see his wife or six children again after he was 'withdrawn from' during the purge that accompanied the rise to power of Jim Taylor Jnr's successor, 'Big Jim' Symington, in the early 70s.

Ian Gibb, a Scottish brother, describes Taylor Junior's rule: 'It was the start of a change from a strict, joyless form of Christianity to a brutal dictatorship. I was 12 years old at the time, but remember the furious arguments – reports almost weekly of meetings dividing, leading men being excommunicated'[102].

The low-point of Jim Taylor Jnr's reign came in 1970 in what became known as the Aberdeen Incident, where Taylor was not only drunk and used grossly indecent language publicly at a three-day meeting, but was also caught in bed with another brother's wife. The incident was reported, not just among the believers, but in the secular press, and it took all the efforts of the Exclusive Brethren's publicity machine to put out the fires. Eventually, Taylor enforced his 'version' of the episode upon the Exclusives, claiming that it was a cunningly devised test of loyalty to identify and root out those who were not truly faithful, to purify the brethren of 'conflicting spirits, silent opposition and rivalry'.

We will not go any further with the shameful story of the Exclusive Brethren. The reason why the story needs to be told, however, is because we are only human beings too, and the same desires – for power, for control through legalism, and for division – still tempt us today. But notice: all three Exclusive principles of separation, dictatorship, and legalism stand in direct contradiction to the biblical principle of love:

1. Darby's principle of separation from evil is not God's principle of unity. It is instead a recipe for endless division over trivial disputes. It is the exact opposite of the true principle of Christian unity: love for all who are truly Christ's.
2. Ignoring the biblical pattern of leadership inevitably leads to dangers. Here, it led to dictatorship by men who seemed very unlike our Lord Jesus Christ. The Exclusive dictatorial system of leadership was the opposite of true spiritual leadership, which is based on love and shepherd care for God's people.
3. Adding to the Bible all sorts of man-made rules, the Exclusives became slaves to legalism. This is the

opposite of true Christianity liberty, in which we can follow our conscience on secondary questions while showing grace and tolerance to others with different views (Romans 14, 1 Cor. 8-10). This is the path of love, instead of legalism.

True Love

Love is a church principle. Having seen the perverted distortion of Christianity the Exclusive Brethren produced when they turned away from biblical principles of Christian fellowship, leadership and scriptural authority we need to finally consider the practical ways in which love can be shown in a local church setting.

The New Testament is full of scriptures that tell us about the importance of love. This is because love is centrally important in the life of the Christian and the church. Here are ten ways we can show love to others:

1. Be Hospitable. When visitors turn up at your assembly on Sunday, have them home to dinner. This is not just a job for the elders (1 Tim. 3:2), nor should we just do it for new visitors or long-time friends from distant towns. We should also be hospitable to members of our own fellowship. Peter writes, 'Be hospitable to one another without grumbling' (1 Pet. 4:9).
2. Share. Just like the early church had 'all things common', it is possible for believers today to share what they have with other Christians in need. Thus, when one believer says to another, 'Here, use our car', we are seeing exactly the same principle in action.

3. Bear one another's burdens (Gal. 6:2), the heavy loads that some have to carry. We can come alongside and help others by listening patiently to their problems, encouraging them in Christ, and going out of our way to do things that help lessen the load for them.
4. Be patient. In Ephesians 4:2 we are told to live 'with all lowliness and gentleness, with longsuffering, bearing with one another in love'. This means we need to bear with the irritating habits of other Christians.
5. Forgive. Forgiveness is hard, but the Bible gives us a good reason why we should forgive: 'be kind to one another, tenderhearted, forgiving one another, just as God in Christ forgave you' (Eph. 4:32).
6. Stop judging others. In 1 Corinthians 8-10 and Romans 14-15, Paul writes about how it is normal for Christians to have different opinions on some secondary matters of spirituality. For example, some Christians had different opinions about holding some days special, or about eating food offered to idols. But he says, 'why do you judge your brother? Or why do you show contempt for your brother? For we shall all stand before the judgment seat of Christ' (Rom. 14:10). Some Christians were judging others for doing things they did not approve of, while in return others despised those who, in all good conscience, felt unable to do certain things. Either way, we should 'live and let live', allowing others to follow their conscience, because we know that we are not the judges of our brothers and sisters – the Lord is.

7. Wash one another's feet (John 13, 1 Tim. 5:10). In John 13, the Lord taught us to wash one another's feet, and He told Peter, 'what I am doing you do not understand now, but you will know after this' (John 13:7). In John 15:3 he explained His meaning, 'You are already clean because of the word which I have spoken to you'. The ultimate service of love we can perform for others is to share God's Word with them, which purifies them in the same way that Christ does the church: 'that He might sanctify and cleanse her with the washing of water by the word' (Eph. 5:26).
8. Pray for each other (James 5:16).
9. Serve others in love. In Galatians 5:13-15, Paul urges us to 'through love serve one another', and warns 'but if you bite and devour one another, beware lest you be consumed by one another'. Here we have love's action and legalism's bitter fruit.
10. Submit to others. Don't always insist on things being done your way, as if you were infallible and no one else ever had a better idea. Peter says, 'all of you be submissive to one another, and be clothed with humility, for "God resists the proud, but gives grace to the humble"' (1 Peter 5:5).

Paul concludes his first letter to the Corinthians with the words, 'Let all that you do be done with love' (1 Cor. 16:14). He concludes his second letter to them with these words: 'Be of good comfort, be of one mind, live in peace, and the God of love and peace will be with you' (2 Cor. 13:11).

Chapter Ten

CONCLUSION

Brethren assemblies in the West are dying. Yet God's desire is always to revive His work. He promises that if His people turn back to Him in repentance and prayer, He will do this.

I have suggested there are four main reasons for the decline and five principles for blessing and growth. Here, in time-honoured Brethren tradition, they are listed in alliterative outline.

The four main reasons for decline are:

1. Lack of healthy teaching when 'the whole church comes together' (1 Cor. 14:23), instead relegating teaching to a time when many of the most spiritually needy and struggling are not able or willing to attend.
2. Leadership problems, in particular the lack of shepherd-like care and feeding of the flock, privately as well publicly.
3. Legalism rather than love. Christianity is about the power of love rather than the love of power.
4. Lack of training for the next generation, particularly in raising up future full-time workers to go into struggling assemblies and revive them.

On the other hand, there is only one way that revival of God's work ever happens, throughout Scripture or Christian history: by God's people turning to Him again with all their heart, in humble repentance and believing prayer. God only needs a few people who are totally committed to His cause, who will trust His Word and obey His commands, and He will do great things again through them.

The five principles for seeing God's work revived are:

1. The Power of God's Spirit – not by relying on our own ingenuity or organization or education or finances, or by following trendy new fads.
2. Prayer: God's people need to put aside other things and come together before Him in repentant, believing prayer. Believing prayer means praying specifically, expectantly, persistently, sacrificially and earnestly.
3. Personal godliness: walking with the Lord every day, being filled with His Spirit.
4. Preaching the gospel, making contact with unsaved people and boldly sharing the message of Christ with them, privately and publicly.
5. Participatory church gatherings (alongside expository preaching), overseen by godly shepherds who not only feed the flock themselves, but stir up others' gifts and guide those not gifted in public preaching into other areas of Christian service. Participatory church gatherings are important, not only because Christians grow by involvement – by using their gifts interactively in the church – but also because we need to allow the Holy Spirit to work inside the church as well as depending upon Him in our evangelistic outreach in the world.

ENDNOTES

[1] "Who are the Brethren" pamphlet, quoted by Ian McDowell, *A Brief History of the "Brethren"*, Victory Books, 1968, pp55-56

[2] Roy Hill, *What is Happening to UK Assemblies? 2005*, https://plymouthbrethren.org/article/1707

[3] *The Brethren Movement Worldwide, Key Information 2019*, eds. Ken & Jeanette Newton, 5th ed. Opal, IBCM, 2019, p333

[4] Alan F. Dyer, *God was their Rock*, Pioneer, 1974

[5] Since 2015, lists of assemblies in Australia have been kept by CCCAust, a broader grouping of churches than just Brethren assemblies, and with the incorporation of other types of churches, numbers have risen. Some of these churches might be surprised to be told they are counted as Brethren!

[6] *The Brethren Movement Worldwide, Key Information 2019*, eds. Ken & Jeanette Newton, 5th ed. Opal, IBCM, 2019

[7] Thus, in the USA, Brethrenpedia listed 806 assemblies in 2018 (https://brethrenpedia.org/index.php/USA_Assembly_Number_Stats), but there were 834 assemblies according to the Emmaus 2022 Assemblies Address book (my count). Similarly, in Canada, the numbers increased over these years from 438 to 452.

[8] Alexander Kurian, *The Decline of the Assemblies: Is the Revival Movement in Need of a Revival?*, https://www.alexkurian.org/thedeclineoftheassemblies

[9] Tim Grass, *Gathering to His Name*, Paternoster, 2006, p287

[10] Taken from the Church Growth Modelling website, https://churchmodel.org.uk/2022/05/15/growth-decline-and-extinction-of-uk-churches/, which bases its figures on data from Brierley Consultancy (UK Church Statistics). The different churches are, from left to right: Welsh Presbyterian, United Reformed, Church in Wales, Welsh Independents,

Roman Catholic Church, Methodists, Church of Scotland, Church of England, Baptists, Salvation Army, Open Brethren, Free Church of Scotland, Seventh Day Adventist, Elim, New Frontiers, FIEC, Vineyard.

[11] Groves, *Memoir*, p49, quoted in G. H. Lang, *Anthony Norris Groves*, 1949, p105

[12] Darby, *Letters*, 1.18, April 1833

[13] Darby, Letter in 1839

[14] quoted in Harry Ironside, *Historical Sketch of the Brethren Movement*, Loizeaux, 1988, p79-80

[15] Blair Neatby, *A History of the Plymouth Brethren*, 1902, p29

[16] Ian McDowell, *A Brief History of the Brethren*, P48

[17] Groves, Memoir, quoted in Lang, p173-4

[18] Tim Grass, *Gathering to His Name*, Paternoster, p13

[19] R. B. Dann, *Father of Faith Missions: the Life and Times of Anthony Norris Groves*, Paternoster, 2004, p13

[20] Roy Coad, *A History of the Brethren Movement*, Paternoster, 1968, p261

[21] William MacDonald, *True Discipleship*, p5

[22] Darby, *Letters*, 3.297

[23] Dann, *Father of Faith Mission*, p199

[24] Henry Groves, *Not of the World: A Memoir of Lord Congleton*, John F. Shaw and Co., 1884, p15

[25] C. H. Mackintosh, "The Bible: Its Sufficiency and Supremacy" in *The Mackintosh Treasury: Miscellaneous Writings*, Neptune, NJ: Loizeaux Brothers, 1976, p17, 20

[26] Emma Frances Bevan, *The Gospel According to Paul*, 1894

[27] *Collected Writings of J. N. Darby*, Ecclesiastical, Vol. 1, p49

[28] R. B. Dann, *Father of Faith Missions, the Life and Times of Anthony Norris Groves*, p50

[29] *Household Words*, a Weekly Journal by Charles Dickens, November 7, 1857.

[30] George Müller, *Narrative of the Lord's Dealings*, 1.276-81

[31] Dann, *Father of Faith Missions*, p509
[32] Ken Newton and Andrew Chan, *To the Ends of the Earth*, AMT, 2010, p9
[33] Ken Newton, "Seeing the Bible Through Mission Eyes", in Harold H. Rowdon (ed.), *The Brethren Contribution to the Worldwide Mission of the Church: International Brethren Conference on Mission, 1993* (Carlisle: Paternoster for Partnership, 1994), p13
[34] Anne Arnott, *The Brethren, an Autobiography of a Plymouth Brethren Childhood*, Mowbray, 1969, p182
[35] Neatby, *History of the Plymouth Brethren*, p339
[36] Neatby, *History*, p3
[37] According to Burridge, see Grass, *Gathering*, p168
[38] Lifeway Research (2016) surveyed 1000 Protestant senior pastors in the USA. 36% believe the Lord will come and rapture the church before the Great Tribulation, 18% believe He will come and rapture the church after the Great Tribulation, 8% believe the rapture occurs midway through the tribulation period, 25% say that there is no such thing as a literal rapture, 8% do not agree with any of these views, and 4% are not sure.
[39] H. A. Ironside, *Historical Sketch of the Brethren Movement*, Grand Rapids, MI: Zondervan, 1942, pp211-12.
[40] Coad, *History of the Brethren Movement*, p172
[41] Dann, *Father of Faith Missions*, p560
[42] Grass suggests that of the total Brethren (132), another one-third more were not labelled as Brethren (=175), plus others which did not submit returns (~200), of which two-thirds were open (125), see *Gathering to His Name*, p115-6.
[43] Alexander Kurian, *The Decline of the Assemblies*
[44] William MacDonald, "It's Time We Faced The Facts: Why is the Church Powerless?" reprinted in *Cornerstone* magazine, Nov 2017, https://cornerstonemagazine.org/its-time-we-faced-the-facts-why-is-the-church-powerless/

[45] Nathan Delynn Smith, *Roots, Renewal and the Brethren*, Pasadena, CA: Hope, 1986, pp101-125

[46] A. Rendle-Short, *Principles*, p121

[47] J. R. Green, *A Short History of the English People*, Harper, 1899, p736-7

[48] Or, better, administration, i.e. godly order in the church.

[49] William MacDonald, *Believers Bible Commentary*, Nashville, TN: Thomas Nelson, 1995, p1801

[50] Leon Morris, *1 Corinthians*, TNTC, IVP, 1985, p190

[51] G. D. Fee, *The First Epistle to the Corinthians*, NICNT, Eerdmans, 1987, p691

[52] I. H. Marshall, "1 Thessalonians", *New Bible Commentary*, 4th Ed., IVP, 1994, p1284

[53] F. F. Bruce, *1 and 2 Corinthians*, NCBC, Marshall, Morgan and Scott, 1971, p135.

[54] A. Rendle-Short, *Principles*, p99

[55] Grass, *Gathering*, pp219-220

[56] Coad, *History*, p179-80

[57] Grattan Guinness, *A Letter to the "Plymouth Brethren" on the Recognition of Pastors*, 1863

[58] Grass, *Gathering*, p69

[59] Grass, *Gathering*, p69

[60] See Ironside, *Historical Sketch*, p40

[61] Dann, *Father of Faith Missions*, p404-5

[62] Dr. William McRae, *The Meeting of the Church*, Dallas: Believers Chapel, 1974, 2001.

[63] David Wells, *The Bleeding of the Evangelical Church*, Edinburgh: Banner of Truth, 1995, p8, emphasis in original

[64] D. M. Lloyd-Jones, *Knowing the Times*, Edinburgh: Banner of Truth Trust, 1989, pp195-196

[65] Colin Marshall, *Passing the Baton: A Handbook for Ministry Apprenticeship*, Matthias Media, 2007, p16

[66] Colin Marshall, *Passing the Baton*, back cover.

[67] J. Edwin Orr, *The Second Evangelical Awakening in Britain*, Marshall Morgan and Scott, 1949, p39

[68] See, for example, J. L. Mayhew and Pamela C. Salm, "Gender differences in anaerobic power tests", *European Journal of Applied Physiology and Occupational Physiology*, 60, 1990, pp133–138

[69] F. F. Bruce, *New Century Bible Commentary on 1 and 2 Corinthians*, p104

[70] ibid, p135

[71] J. N. Darby, *Synopsis of the Books of the Bible*, footnote to 1 Cor. 11:2-16

[72] William MacDonald, *Believers Bible Commentary*, Nelson, 1995, p 1785

[73] D. W. Gooding, *Paul's Teaching about Women in 1 Corinthians Chapters 11 and 14*, Belfast: Myrtlefield House, 2019, p4, 6

[74] William Kelly, *Notes on the First Epistle to the Corinthians*, London: G. Morrish, 1878, W. E. Vine, *First Corinthians*, Oliphants, 1951, p147, F. B. Hole, *Old and New Testament Commentary*, W. Hoste, *Bible Problems and Answers*, ed. Wm. Bunting, Kilmarnock: John Ritchie, 1957, p326, Alexander Strauch, *Biblical Eldership*, Littleton, CO: Lewis and Roth, 2nd ed, 1988, p221, Malcolm Horlock, "Studies in 1 Corinthians 14, Appendix", *Precious Seed*, Volume 58 Issue 4, 2003, J. M. Riddle, *1 Corinthians*, Kilmarnock: John Ritchie, 2018, p213 (the last two works present this explanation as an option).

[75] Adolf Schlatter, *Paulus der Bote Jesu*, Stuttgart: Calwer, 1969, p390. Philipp Bachmann, *Der erste Brief des Paulus an die Korinther*, Leipzig: Deichert, 1905, pp345-62, R. C. H. Lenski, *1 and 2 Corinthians*, Augsburg Fortress, 1963, pp436-7.

[76] B. B. Warfield, "Paul on Women Speaking in Church", *The Presbyterian*, October 30, 1919

[77] A. Oepke, G. Kittel and G. Friedrich, ed., *Theological*

Dictionary of the New Testament, III, pp561-3

[78] verse 15b in the AV does not mention long hair, however 'long hair' is indeed the best translation of the Greek word *kome* used in v15b. It is the same word used for 'long hair' in the first part of the verse. Darby and the NIV correctly translate the phrase here using 'long hair'.

[79] Raymond Collins, *First Corinthians*, The Liturgical Press, 1999, pp396-401

[80] Richard Horsley, *1 Corinthians*, Abingdon, 1998, p152

[81] William J. Martin, "1 Corinthians 11:2-16: An Interpretation", in *Apostolic History and the Gospel: Biblical and Historical Essays Presented to F. F. Bruce*, eds. W. W. Gasque and R. P. Martin, Exeter: Paternoster Press, 1970, p233

[82] Phillip Jensen, "The Relationship that is Dependent", sermon delivered at University of New South Wales, 1988, https://phillipjensen.com/resources/the-relationship-that-is-dependent/, Paul Barnett, *1 Corinthians: Holiness and Hope of a Rescued People*, Fearn: Christian Focus, 2000, p197ff., David Pawson, *Unlocking the Bible*, Collins, 2007, p965, Richard Hays, *First Corinthians*, John Knox, 1997, p182, Jerome Murphy-O'Connor, *1 Corinthians*, Veritas, 1979, p107, *1 Corinthians*, The Bible Reading Fellowship, 1999, p126, Stephan Lösch, "Christliche Frauen in Korinth [I Cor. 11:2-16] Ein neuer Lösungsversuch" *ThQ* 127 (1947), pp216-267, Elizabeth Schüssler Fiorenza, *In Memory of Her*, Crossroad/Herder & Herder, 1994, pp227-8, J. B. Hurley, *Man and Woman in Biblical Perspective*, Zondervan, 1981, Abel Isaksson, *Marriage and Ministry in the New Temple: a Study with Special Reference to Mt. 19:13-12 [sic] and 1 Cor. 11:2-16*, Lund: Gleerup, 1965

[83] David Pawson, *Unlocking the Bible*, p965. The only item of clothing mentioned in the passage is in the last verse, where 'veil' literally means a 'cloak' (Gk. *peribolaion*). The Greek

preposition *anti* is correctly translated as 'instead of' (as virtually everywhere else in NT). For more on this verse and the subject, see the author's book, *Ten Myths about Headship and Head Covering: The Truth of 1 Corinthians 11:2-16*.

[84] Nathan Smith, *Roots, Renewal and the Brethren*, p47-8

[85] Alexander Kurian, *The Decline of the Assemblies*

[86] John R. W. Stott, *The Message of Ephesians*, BST, Nottingham: IVP, 1979, 1989, p167

[87] Stephen S. Short, "The Ministry of the Word", *The Witness*, February 1965, p43

[88] Alexander Strauch, *Biblical Eldership*, Lewis & Roth, 1988, pp12-13

[89] Lightfoot, *The Christian Ministry*, The Epistles of St. Paul: Philippians, 4th Ed., London, Macmillan and Co., 1879, p186-87, 201. Leon Morris, 'Church Government', in *Encyclopedia of Christianity*, Vol. 2, 484

[90] John Riddle, *Acts*, John Ritchie, 2012, p229

[91] Nathan Smith, *Roots*, p48

[92] Ibid, p48

[93] Alex Kurian, *The Decline of the Assemblies*

[94] George Barna, *Habits of Highly Effective Churches*, pp30-31

[95] Alex Kurian, *The Decline of the Assemblies*

[96] H. A. Ironside, *A Historical Sketch of the Brethren Movement*, Loizeaux Brothers, 1985, p83

[97] Ironside, *Historical Sketch*, p85

[98] Ironside, p89

[99] Michael Bachelard, *Behind the Exclusive Brethren*, Melbourne: Scribe, 2008, pp31-32

[100] W.R. Dronsfield, 'The Brethren Since 1870', www.biblecentre.org/ topics/wrd_brethren_since_1870.htm

[101] Bachelard, *Behind the Exclusive Brethren*, p34

[102] Ibid.

www.ingramcontent.com/pod-product-compliance
Lightning Source LLC
Chambersburg PA
CBHW030435010526
44118CB00011B/645